THE PHILOSOPHY OF LOKĀYATA

Some other Books by the Same Author

1. Secularism and National Integration (ed.)
2. Reflection on Buddhism
3. Ethics, Language and Tradition (ed.)
4. Reflections on Indian Wisdom (ed.)
5. Analysis in Śaṅkara Vedānta (ed.)
6. Dharma, Darshana O' Mānavatāvāda (Oḍiyā)
7. Sāṅkhya Darshana (Oḍiyā)
8. The Sāṅkhya Philosophy: An Analytical Study
9. Value Perspectives in Indian Philosophy
10. Indian Philosophy: An Analytical Study
11. The Theories of Error in Indian Philosophy
12. Bauddhica Saṅkaṭa (Oḍiyā)
13. Major Trends in Orissan Philosophy
14. Dārshanika Nīlakaṇṭha (Oḍiyā) (ed.)
15. Sri Aurobindo and Spritualistic Humanism
16. The Humanist Vision

THE PHILOSOPHY OF LOKĀYATA

A Review and Reconstruction

BIJAYANANDA KAR

MOTILAL BANARSIDASS PUBLISHERS
PRIVATE LIMITED • DELHI (INDIA)

2nd Corrected Edition: Delhi, 2017
First Edition: Delhi, 2013

ISBN: 978-81-208-3692-1 (Cloth)
ISBN: 978-81-208-4070-6 (Paper)

MOTILAL BANARSIDASS
41 U.A. Bungalow Road, Jawahar Nagar, Delhi 110 007
8 Mahalaxmi Chamber, 22 Bhulabhai Desai Road, Mumbai 400 026
203 Royapettah High Road, Mylapore, Chennai 600 004
236, 9th Main III Block, Jayanagar, Bengaluru 560 011
8 Camac Street, Kolkata 700 017
Ashok Rajpath, Patna 800 004
Chowk, Varanasi 221 001

Printed in India

by RP Jain at NAB Printing Unit,
A-44, Naraina Industrial Area, Phase I, New Delhi–110028
and published by JP Jain for Motilal Banarsidass Publishers (P) Ltd,
41 U.A. Bungalow Road, Jawahar Nagar, Delhi-110007

CONTENTS

PREFACE

It is needless to point out that the philosophy of Cārvāka has been dealt with a cursory treatment in traditional Indian philosophical literature. Even in modern writings, there are (barring few exceptions) not much philosophical probing to bring to focus the logical foundation of the Cārvāka point of view. Paucity of original source-material is, of course, an impediment for such investigation. But, nevertheless, attempts have been made by few researchers to present a viable account of the Cārvāka stand, scanning out the unsound filthy observations, especially made by the opponents.

Since my early days of taking up Indian philosophy, I continue to have the feeling of discomfort while enquiring about the philosophical position of Cārvāka. The accounts that are now available are not convincing and I was all along keen to find an opportunity to have a detailed review of the philosophy of Cārvāka.

I became happy when I was offered Senior Fellowship by the Indian Council of Philosophical Research (ICPR) on a project (submitted by me) on Cārvāka with a view to reconstruct and to have a fresh evaluation of the same, keeping due regard of its contemporary relevance. I am grateful to ICPR for necessary financial support in this regard.

From the available source-materials, it is found that the Cārvākas have some points to offer with regard to the major issues like knowledge, belief, dogma, the concept of God, soul and morality in the socio-human empirical framework. I have made an effort to analyze the issues in the light of the Cārvākian standpoint. To me it appears that the reading of materialism in respect of the philosophy of Cārvāka definitely needs reconsideration. In the present work, I have placed my reasons against the materialistic rendering of the Cārvāka stand.

I take this opportunity to thank Dr. (Mrs.) Namita Kar, Dr. Saroj Kanta Kar, Shree Naba Kishore Pujari, Dr. Sudhakar Jally and Miss Sravani Satpathy who have ungrudgingly helped me in processing the whole manuscript through computer and checking carefully the errors of omission and commission as well. Whatever lapse is left out, I am solely responsible.

I would feel rewarded if the learned readers will offer their remarks and suggestions for my further reflection on the subject.

AM-26, VSS Nagar
Bhubaneswar-721007

Bijayananda Kar

INTRODUCTION

The Cārvāka/Lokāyata *darśana* is found to have a notable place in the classical Indian philosophical tradition. Its reference is found in the earliest sources like the Vedas/Upaniṣads, the Buddhist *suttas*, the Jaina treatises, the *Rāmāyaṇa* and the *Mahābhārata*, inclusive of some purāṇic and śāstric works. It goes without saying that, by and large, such references mostly present a very negative and damaging account of the Cārvāka point of view. From such sources, certain aphorisms (*sūtras*) are cited as the composition of the founder of the Cārvāka *darśana*, Bṛhaspati.

The name is not found to refer to one single person. There are two different individuals, having two distinct views, referred to in the Vedic source. The Vedic hymn (X.71, X.72) refers to Bṛhaspati Aṅgirasa and Bṛhaspati Laukya. The former is said to be the priest (*purohita*) of devas (including Indra) and the latter may possibly be pointing to another person who is represented as instructor to the demons. This point is confirmed when in the later *Maitrāyaṇa Upaniṣad* it is held that Bṛhaspati is none other than Śukrācārya, the priest and instructor of demons (*asuras*). It is quite likely that in order to downgrade the contribution of the Cārvāka point of view, there was the attempt in some of the Upaniṣadic sources to vilify Bṛhaspati as the instructor of demons, instead of gods. It is notable that amidst number of different references about Bṛhaspati, it is plausible that in the name, Bṛhaspati there are number of persons (not one) and mainly one is acclaimed as *deva guru* and the other is *dānava guru*.

The aphorisms, attributed to Bṛhaspati are neither found to be complete (in the sense of comprising one full text) nor are those noticed to be coherently contiguous. Moreover, since those aphorisms are collected from different sources, those do not at the outset at least exhibit any systematic pattern of thought. For instance, on one occasion it is stated that sense-perception is the only source of knowledge (*pratyakṣameva pramāṇaṁ*) and in another case it is stated that sense-perception is the source of knowledge (*pratyakṣamaikya pramāṇaṁ*).[1] Furthermore, because most of the references are traced from the opponent and unsympathetic sources, the presentation is explicitly biased, distorted and even spurious. At least, this is more or less the legitimate apprehension of some notable modern scholars. Incidentally, only one full text: *Tattvapaplava-siṁha*, composed by Jayarāsi (800 CE) is now available and it is taken as a treatise on the Cārvāka *darśana.*

But, again, there is no unanimity on this reading. Some think this work as an independent text and not belonging to the Cārvāka standpoint on account of its being sceptical about all sources of knowledge, including sense-perception. However, it is worth-noting that Jayaraāsi himself clearly acknowledged and referred to Bṛhaspati as his mentor (*guru*) in his text. And, despite the sceptical tone in the epistemological front, there are certain conspicuous similarities between the view-point of Jayarāsi and the view that is in general ascribed to the Cārvākas. It is noticed that some pre-Buddhists, known as the Ājivakas (referred to in the Early Buddhist *suttas*) are found to be quite close (if not fully identical) to the Cārvākas in the sense, those thinkers did not advocate any form of supernaturalism or transcendentalism. Some of them were designated as naturalists (*svabhāvavādins*), non-actionists (*akriyāvādins*) and chance-mechanists (*yadṛchāvādins*), instead of clearly being labelled as materialists. Anyway, their view-points have certain resemblance with the Cārvāka point of view.

1. *Vide* Bhattacharya, R.K. Cārvāka Aphorisms in *The Journal of Indian Philosophy,* Vol. XXX, No. 6, 2002-2003.

In this context, there is another interesting point of reference. Kauṭilya (the famous writer of the great classic text: *Arthaśāstra - 300/400BCE*) mentioned only three *darśanas* in which Lokāyata (Cārvāka) was mentioned along with Sāṅkhya and Yoga, with clear omission of Veda as well as Vedānta. The ground that was offered by Kauṭilya is very pertinent. It was held that reason (*hetu*) in some way or other was the basis of arriving at a philosophic standpoint. In other words, nothing which is not based on reason and is solely founded on hearsay, prejudice and tradition was not considered by him as *ānvīkṣikī* (*darśana*), i.e., critical enquiry. The Cārvākas questioned the dogmatic acceptance of tradition, despite its being strongly rooted in the psyche especially of the elites. Their emphasis on reasoning was, in subsequent period, criticized by the opponents and they, as rationalists (*haitukas*) were labelled (of course, misleadingly) as condemner of the Vedas (*Veda virodhīnaḥ tarka vyavahāriṇaḥ*).

The Cārvāka view-point, presented as anti-Vedic, is notably founded in the traditional sources. For instance, in the *Ramāyaṇa* the Cārvākas are depicted as the top heretic (*nāstika śiromaṇiḥ*). The same point is again echoed in Manu's characterization of the heterodox ones as hater of the Vedas (*nāstiko Veda nindakaḥ*). But, this sort of unfair treatment of the Cārvāka point of view definitely deserves reconsideration. Even if it is noticed from some of the references (attributed to the Cārvākas) that they are critical about the Vedic sources, it has to be understood contextually, never ignoring that. Only when certain Vedic utterances point to the acceptance of supra-empirical or transcendental entities like disembodied self/soul/spirit (*dehātirikta ātmā*), heaven (*svarga*), hell (*narka*) etc. as really existent and such Vedic utterances are treated as inviolable truths and self-valid (*svataḥ prāmāṇya*) without any justification, the logical implication of the Cārvāka point of view becomes explicit in being critical about such dogmatic and prejudiced stand. There is, of course, no wholesale condemnation of the Vedic source as such in an outright procedure. In fact the Vedic line which is found to be in accordance with the Cārvāka view-point (*dṛṣṭi*) and is fairly reasonable, that is never set aside.[2] Their critical reflection on certain Vedic expressions requires to be evaluated contextually as per the generally accepted principle of reason. It is interesting to note that even the Mīmāṁsakas (both *pūrva* and *uttara*) have never also opted for wholesale, unconditional acceptance of the Vedic sayings but only have selected those that suit their respective philosophical stand and their interpretation follows that procedure quite consistently. From this point of view, even the Cārvākian standpoint need not be swallowed unreflectively without the aid of reason. At least the logical tone of the Cārvāka position cannot accommodate that. That is why it takes recourse to reason and it is duly recognized by Kauṭilya. Even the opponents (as indicated before) admitted that; but they, on account of their deep-seated dogmatic conservative bias could not move along with reason and remained bound within the confinement of mystical obscurity in some form or other.

In a later Buddhist treatise: *Tattvasaṅgraha* by Śāntarakṣita (700 CE) which is commented upon by Kamalaśīla (*Pañjikā*), there is a clear reference to one Cārvāka, named as Purandara who, it is stated, accepted inference (*anumāna*) in a reasonably specific sense over and above sense-perception. Purandara's own writing is not now found, though his view (which is no doubt very significant in the context of Cārvāka philosophy) is referred to in the cited source.

Long after (1400 CE), Mādhavācārya brought out one compendium: *Sarva darśana saṅgraha* in which there is more or less an elaborate account of the Cārvāka point of view. Besides, there are also other works of compilation like *Ṣaḍ darśana samuccaya* which mention the Cārvāka view, not withstanding references noticed in *smṛtis, purāṇas* inclusive of the Buddhist and the Jaina

2. *Vide*, in this connection, Sadānanda: *Vedāntasāra* where he referred to the Vedic source that is acceptable to the Cārvāka stand.

sources. However, it is to be conceded that such works are only compilations, not the work of any Cārvāka thinker as such.

The Cārvāka position, it is said, goes against social order. It moves beyond the social classification (*varṇa-vyavasthā*). The four-fold classification of men (*puruṣa* into *catur-varṇa*) which has its indication in *Ṛg Veda* and is made more explicit subsequently in the *Bh. Gītā* is not admitted in the Cārvākian framework. But the non-acceptance of the four-fold classification of men-in-society need not necessarily warrant the dismissal of the social order as such. The rejection of such division can be traced to other factors, without dismantling the functioning of the social system. No social convention/custom or rule is sacrosanct and unalterable. It is definitely liable to change and modification, if the situation so demands. Classification of men-in-society for some legitimate purpose and requirement is not after all one unwelcome move. But that need not be thought as absolute and incorrigible. In a changing set up, the social classification demands review. In this sense, it need not be confined to a closed circle, but it requires to be considered liberally in terms of open-mindedness.

Again, the theological boosting of the four-fold classification (as is done in the tradition of *Bh. Gītā*) is never prone to reason. It definitely encroaches upon the autonomy of morality in the social plane by way of insisting on unwarranted theological supremacy. The logic of the Cārvāka stand seems to be on the solid ground in abstaining itself from such baseless dogmatic tradition. Actually, in that way, it does not upset the social order, but rather questions effectively the ill-grounded, unjustified trans-social classification of people.

The Cārvāka view-point has been criticized in different sources (both classical and modern) insofar as it is alleged to have prompted gross hedonist outlook by way of advocating utter sensualism, sexualism and baser joys and pleasure. It promotes devilish features.

It is remarked that by way of emphasising on the sensual desire (*kāma*) and putting even wealth (*artha*) on the secondary level (that is, one can take recourse to borrowing money, if one does not originally possess it and can enjoy the living in the satisfying form), the Cārvāka stand, it is said, turns out to be irrational. It is also much away from morality (*dharma*) according to the critics. Further, it is absolutely incapable of comprehending the highest or supreme value in human life (*mukti/mokṣa*).[3] Consequently, a Cārvāka is characterised as impostor (*pākhanḍaḥ*), sinner (*pāpī*), heretic (*nāstika*), womanizer (*strī-lampaṭa*), ill-mannerly (*durācāra*), ungrateful (*kṛtaghna*), rougue (*vakrabṛttayaḥ*), unduty-bound (*karmabhraṣṭa*) and destitute of forgiveness (*kṣamanasta*). He is ridiculed as indulging in useless discussion, and is a gross sensualist, angry, violent, cheater and is devoid of knowledge.[4]

No doubt, if these characterizations have some basis, then the stand of Cārvāka can hardly be defended. Not only such a stand goes against reason, it is also most impractical in the socio-individual plane. The non-availability of adequate amount of original or authentic sources stands as an impediment either to affirm or to negate the criticisms satisfactorily. Unlike the other classical Indian philosophies, the Cārvāka view-point is not found to be presented in any classical text in a systematic form. Any commentary/digest/gloss on the Cārvāka source material is not available. Only there are some scattered ideas and thoughts, loosely knitted together in some aphorisms found available from different sources. But, all the same, there is one remarkable point which need not be overlooked. Almost all the other *darśanas* (as indicated before) have referred to Cārvāka as the opponent and, after discarding the opponent's stand (not

3. *Vide* Prasad, S.N.: *Chārvāka/Lokāyata— Analytic and Hermeneutic Study* (Patna: Janaki Prakashan, 2008), p. 38. However, Prasad has later specified the sense in which Cārvāka is castigated and ridiculed as anti-dharmic (*dharma virodhī*), *ibid.*, p.112.
4. *Vide* Guru-gītā in *Skanda Purāṇa* (also referred to by Prasad, *ibid.*, 137)

necessarily by means of advancing any rational argument), those try to establish their respective stand. That means, the Cārvāka point of view, by and large, is rather extruded than exploded. This reveals that the Cārvāka view is not simply a view of antiquity and since long it is outdated, but, on the contrary, it is a continuous living point of view, again and again lurking in the Indian philosophical circle being referred to and being discussed. Again, the view is obviously current in the ordinary popular circle, quite in tune with the connotation of the other accepted synonym of the term i.e., Lokāyata.

It is, of course, the case that the Cārvāka philosophic stand has not been systematically presented in the classical phase. But, taking into due consideration of the stray passages that are found available both in the aphorisms (attributed to the Cārvāka stand) and also the ideas and views identified as belonging to Cārvāka (in the opponent's presentation), it is not entirely fruitless, I suppose, to advance a review as well as reconstruction of the whole standpoint and revaluation of Cārvāka which is definitely alive in the Indian philosophical debate and discussion. In such a process of enquiry the methodology that needs emphasis is obviously analytical and critical. It requires to be based on the general sense of reason that is both theoretically and practically cogent.

Quite a good number of works on Cārvāka philosophical position are published in recent past both in English and some major Indian languages. Writers like D.P. Chattopadhyaya (senior), D.R. Shastri, H.P. Shastri, M.V. Krishna, R.K. Bhattacarya, S.N. Prasad, P.P. Gokhale, D. Bhattacarya, S. Pathak, A. Jha and others have contributed notably towards the exposition of the philosophy Cārvāka in modern times. Some foreign scholars like Colebrooke, Tucci, Raipe, Basham, Brodev, Stepanyants etc. are also note-worthy in this regard. They have, in their own ways, explored the Cārvāka philosophical trends. Radhakrishnan, Dasgupta, Sinha, Hiriyanna, Sharma, Datta and Chatterjee have touched upon the Cārvāka *darśana* in their well-known books on Indian philosophy.

Modern writings have more or less tried to present the philosophy of Cārvāka, adopting generally the well established philosophical categorization in terms of exploring its metaphysical, epistemological and ethical/moral perspectives. The impact of the Cārvāka point of view on the socio-cultural level has been discussed in some such sources. R.K. Bhattacharya has made a thorough study of the available Cārvāka *sūtras* and has raised the issue as to which *sūtras* are genuine to the Cārvāka stand and which are not. S.N. Prasad has tried to have a comparative study of the Cārvākian thought with that of Omer Khayyam, D.H. Lawrence and the well-known Hindi poet: H.R. Bachchan.

All such contributions, no doubt, are quite resourceful in their own ways. Some like Brodev has tried to present the Cārvākian thought from the angle of Marxian materialism. Recently, Amartya Sen has remarked that there is a long argumentative tradition in India in which the rational and sceptical approach of the Cārvāka/Lokāyata is significant. It is remarkable that while making diverse appraisal/evaluation of the Cārvāka *darśana* (whether positive or negative), certain amount of construction is, of course, necessary. In some cases (it is needless to point out), the preset mental makeup of the particular writer towards Indian philosophical studies plays a vital role. For instance, Radhakrishnan when wrote about Cārvāka could not appreciate its critical approach on account of his strong leanings towards some form of religious spiritualism. So also the Marxian rendering of the Cārvākian view-point is quite likely due to seeing it through the modern materialistic movement. In the similar pattern, the Cārvāka stand has been read in terms of agnosticism, atheism, commonsense populism, empiricism, existentialism, hedonism, humanism, materialism, mechanism, naturalism, positivism, pragmatism, rationalism (different from anti-empiricistic rationalism), satirism, scepticism, secularism, sensationalism, sensualism, socialism, soft-spokenism and worldism, etc.

But to read any kind of 'ism' exclusively into the Cārvāka standpoint appears to be unfair and problematic. It is because initially the ideas and thoughts which move along with Cārvāka position are noticed to be somewhat discontinuous and those are never woven together to form one complete system or a whole. That means those cannot be put together as such. In order to do that one needs to make some addition/ reconstruction (may be some elimination, if found to be reasonably necessary). And, when that is accomplished, the resultant formulation turns out to be a novel creation. So to hold that such construction is what the original Cārvākas actually asserted or not is, perhaps, one unwarranted claim. At least that cannot be treated as a historical conclusion. Any rereading or interpreting the Cārvāka position (and any other for that matter) need not be construed as digging the past and to discover anything that is factually true like finding an emperor's castle by means of excavation or being informed about certain event of emperor's life by discovering one authoritative inscriptional evidence, etc.

Therefore, review/reappraisal of the Cārvāka stand amounts to a conceptual reconstruction and such presentation need not be evaluated from the point of factual confirmation but from the point of view of rational cogency and coherency. Of course, sometimes both factual and conceptual probing overlaps and creates the impression that as if there is no difference between the two. However, it is notable that the very point of overlapping implies that the two are reasonably distinct and need to be discriminated.

It is advocated (almost taken for granted) that the Cārvāka philosophy is nothing but materialism. It is held that according to the Cārvākas earth, water, air and fire are the primary elements. Basing on that stand it is held that the Cārvāka philosophy affirms a materialistic ontology according to which matter is only real. It alone is existent, primordial constituent of the whole universe.[5] However,

5. *Ibid.*, p.35 (on the basis of Dictionary of *Philosophy* by D.D. Runes)

in view of the Cārvākian standpoint as outspokenly against any trans-empirical and metaphysical construction, any move for reading transcendental metaphysics into the Cārvāka stand definitely needs reconsideration. It is pertinent that the Cārvākian acceptance of four elements is not on the metaphysical basis but on the epistemological ground of sense-empiricism. The four elements are not construed as ultimately real/existent entities, but those are held to be elemental only on the basis of empirical observation.[6] In other words, observation is the determining factor for their acceptance. Those are not accepted on the basis of any trans-empirical speculation from a metaphysical source.

It is maintained that the Cārvāka stand amounts to atheism and is opposed to any form of theism. It goes without saying that the existence of God is implied in theism and that is never admissible to the Cārvāka standpoint. God is presupposed to be transcendental real being and He is supposed to be the creator of the whole universe. On account of non-perceptibility, the existence of God can neither be inferred nor can be supposed without the violation of reasoning so far as the Cārvāka stand is concerned. Since the claim of knowledge is empiric-bound, neither the existence nor the non-existence of any metaphysical reality is warranted from the Cārvāka point of view. From this angle, the philosophical position of Cārvāka, precisely speaking, can be held to be neither theistic nor anti-theistic, but moving beyond such dichotomous position. It can, logically speaking, neither subscribe to metaphysical existence nor metaphysical non-existence of anything whatsoever.

Does it then amount to agnosticism? Locke's advocacy of 'unknown substance' and Kant's reference to 'noumenon' or thing-in-itself are usually cited in this context. Since Locke held that knowledge is confined to sense-experience, it cannot grasp the substance in itself. Therefore, the Lockean substance is only a

6. Those are rather empirical constructs in the conceptual frame. See Cārvāka sūtra *'ṛthivyapatejo vāyuriti tattvāni*

presupposition; it cannot in principle be empirically known. The Lockean view is opposed by the critic on the ground that the Lockean empiricistic stand cannot consistently accommodate any metaphysical presupposition of substance in itself. Hence, to admit 'unknown substance' is logically untenable. On the similar ground, the Kantian reference to noumena over and above phenomena is critically viewed (especially by Hegel). If knowledge is limited to phenomena, then the admittance of noumena as unknown and unknowable remains logically incongruent. In other words, agnosticism in this sense is treated as an untenable philosophical position. What is then the status of the Cārvākian standpoint? Is it one inconsistent stand like that of metaphysical agnosticism?

This is not the case, I suppose. True, the philosophical position of Cārvāka does not commit itself to any form of metaphysical presupposition of the transcendental/trans-empirical sort (be it valid or invalid). Metaphysical speculation does not necessitate, on the part of Cārvāka, the admittance of factuality of the things and beings. It does not either commit to the reverse position of denial of everything so far as actuality is taken into consideration. It does honour a distinction between what is real and what is illusory in the observational plane. Only it never for that moves for any transcendental notion of ultimate or absolute reality or pure existent and *vice versa*. That means, it is never logically bound to draw a bridge between factual and logical frame of reference. No factual conclusion can be derived from a formal, *a priori* speculative premise and *vice versa*. The very conception of absolute or ultimate reality does not necessitate the actual existence/non-existence of that in the empirical plane. So to draw any conclusion about noumena from phenomena is not admissible to the Cārvākian stand. That is the reason why a speculative metaphysical leap towards the existence of *Īśvara* (usually treated as a synonym of God), *ātmā* (self/soul/spirit), *svarga* (heaven) is not admitted in the Cārvākian stand.

To put it differently, their stand virtually amounts to a position free from metaphysical speculation (whether valid or invalid). It never attempts to explore a relation between appearance and reality in the metaphysical sense. The distinction between normal snake and the illusory snake is quite valid. Even if there is no dispute about the actual appearance of the illusory snake, it is never taken as real like normal snake. Rope is decidedly real and the so called snake (that appears) is illusory and there cannot be any legitimate scope of treating both of them either as relatively real or as relatively apparent in contrast to absolute reality of metaphysics. Noumena from the Kantian standpoint, is rather a limiting concept in the conceptual framework without entailing any ontological status. It is plausible therefore to hold that the Cārvākian stand is not bound to admit the position of metaphysical agnosticism as it never opts for any metaphysics in that sense.

So also there seems to be some ground for reviewing the other modern philosophical theories (like existentialism, hedonism, scepticism, sensualism, etc.) insofar as those, attributed to the Cārvāka position. Even if, it is conceded that the Cārvākian stand does not opt for any essentialistic position, it does not also accommodate any metaphysical status to existence, as is appealed by some modern existentialists. Similarly, it is notable that, despite the very approval of pleasure (*sukha*), the Cārvāka position never shows any indication to affirm the goal that pleasure is the only normative standard in the ethical plane.

True, the Cārvākian standpoint is indifferent to any trans-empiric metaphysical theoretic construction. It is definitely critical about that. But from this, it does not imply that it is hostile to any knowledge-formation in the ordinary set up. It does not challenge the usual method and practice adopted in the level of ordinary commonsense (including that of science too) for the attainment of knowledge whatsoever. Only it does not embrace any trans-empiric, imaginative construction (*kalpanā gaurava* - coined by some later Buddhists in their epistemological analysis in a different context) on the basis of trans-rational intuitive mystical trance, far removed from both scientific and reflective intellectual investigation. In this manner, its critical approach is unnecessarily belittled and castigated as sceptical from the pejorative angle.

It is, however, the case that for a Cārvāka there is adequate room for rational enquiry within the bounds of practice/reason/sense insofar as general socio-human necessity is taken into account (not at the cost of ruthless exploitation of the eco system consisting of things and beings). In that way it may not be entirely wrong to locate the traces of favouring humanism, pragmatism, naturalism and also general sense of socialism etc. in the Cārvākian philosophical framework. But, at the same time, it seems to be justified to make a reappraisal of such reading of Cārvāka in terms of modern sophisticated expression 'ism' with all its technical nuances.

The terms: Cārvāka and Lokāyata are found to have been used indiscriminately in the Indian philosophical tradition. In the context of the term: Cārvāka, its derivational meaning has been pursued and attempt has been made to locate a linkage between the derivational meaning and the philosophical sense. Again, in some recent studies, the derivational meaning is contested and the philosophical stand of Cārvāka is viewed from altogether different angles.[7] Cārvāka is looked therein as a satirist instead of a sweet/soft-spoken person. The term 'Lokāyata' is analyzed in terms of its derivational meaning and thereby its philosophical sense of focusing to some form of populism (cautiously evading its pejorative sense) has been highlighted. Whatever that may be, in general, there is more or less unanimity in the philosophical circle at least to use both the expressions (Cārvāka and Lokāyata) interchangeably. In the present work, therefore, the same procedure is adopted to avoid discrepancy.

---

7. Prasad, S.N., *op.cit.,* pp. 65-89.

CĀRVĀKA AND KNOWLEDGE

I. Philosophy and Knowledge

Philosophers, down the ages, have taken interest to investigate into the concept of knowledge. Traditionally, the philosophical enquiry aims to expound the concept as such without referring or even relating it to its different cognate concepts, used in the concrete plane of discourse. 'What is knowledge', in this sense, turns out to be an abstract question, neither of any direct interest/relevance to commonsense nor to science (of any sort). Despite this, the philosophical investigation has its conspicuous presence in the human history and, in some quarters, there has been attempt to define/redefine 'knowledge' and thereby to offer an answer to the question, under reference in a reasonably satisfying flawless manner. Such attempts also at times posit to offer an all pervasive explanation concerning knowledge in terms of theorization. Socratic/Platonic account of knowledge in terms of conception, in contrast to perception is a typical illustration in this context. It has the definite tendency to have stipulation and to offer an explanation of the concept of knowledge in such a manner so that the ordinary commonsense version of knowledge in the empirical plane at least becomes marginalized, if not totally eliminated. Similarly the Vedāntin's account of knowledge (*jñāna*) as pure (*śuddha*), perfect (*parama*), timeless (*kālātīta*) and uncontradicted (*abādhita*) points to stipulation, either lowering the ordinary commonsensical understanding of knowledge as merely workable (in the relative sense) or completely dismissing it as false (*mithyā*). In any case, knowledge is redefined to accommodate the pre-set speculation in the abstract plane.

In the field of epistemology, the philosophers like idealists and realists are found to be sharply opposed to each other with regard to the nature of knowledge. The issue is: whether it is confined to only ideas (subjectivity) or it points to objects, independent of ideas (objectivity). Both the accounts, it can be noted, are on the abstract plane, moving beyond concrete specification. Classical rationalists advocate *a priori* reason as the sole basis of knowledge with an implicit approval of defining knowledge as absolutely apodictic, certain and necessary. The empiricists, on the other hand, advocate experience (sense) as the basis of knowledge conceding that knowledge must be *a posteriori* and novel. Of course, all empiricists do not opt for one single account of experience. But, despite the differences amongst them, it is notable that more or less they are not so much keen to have any pre-set speculative abstract notion of knowledge. They rather try to analyze the concept of knowledge within the concrete empirical framework. Accordingly, those are nearer to commonsense and science. By way of emphasizing the role of sense-experience for the construction of knowledge, they do not, of course, reject the role of reason outright. Reason has its share; but it is never conceived to be the sole arbiter. On the contrary, it is taken up with a view to boost up, regulate and systematize the empirical claim of knowledge.

In the modern period, there has been remarkable change in the philosophical studies. Instead of opting for all-inclusive speculative construction and also somewhat hesitant to remain confined to the bounds of epistemological claim of either rationalism or empiricism, philosophers prefer to analyze the concept of knowledge, taking into account cognate concepts like belief, evidence, justification, probability, truth, validity etc. Instead of moving for a stipulation in redefining the abstract concept: knowledge, they prefer to expose as well as keen to focus the significant manner in which the concept 'knowledge' is operated in the concrete setting. Different philosophical views are formulated with regard to the logico-linguistic status of the concept, by way of analytically reviewing knowledge/knowing as 'capacity', 'performative', 'right to be sure', 'justified belief' 'etc. Subtle distinctions are marked between 'knowing how' and 'knowing that'. All such analytic probing is found to be strikingly different from the classical philosophical enquiry about the concept in the abstract setting. As hinted before, the analytical pursuit is conducted more or less at the concrete factual background. It does not, however, imply that the logico-linguistic conceptual analytical methodology is adopted by all philosophers of repute during the present era. Diversity of approach is very much noticed. But, nevertheless, philosophical activity is found to be predominantly taking due note of its role and impact in the applied concrete situation than just to be engrossed with unworkable speculative surmises.

II. Difficulties

With this brief preliminary survey of the enquiry into 'knowledge' in the realm of philosophy (in general), let there be the move for looking at Cārvāka philosophy. Before advancing any conclusive remark on Cārvāka, one should not overlook the difficulties to locate the position of Cārvāka from a philosophical angle. As already indicated before, there is no authoritative textual evidence to clearly point to one historical person as the founder of the Cārvāka *darśana* (as is usually found to be the case with other classical *darśanas*). Though generally Cārvāka and Lokāyata are treated to be same, it is also held by the scholars that Lokāyata is the original trend of thought and Cārvāka is a later formulation whose first occurrence is noticed in the *Rāmāyaṇa*. There is, of course, non-availability of any original text/treatise on the Cārvākian thought and only the stray references are found from the opponent and other secondary sources. Quite often the views expressed in such sources are noticed to be not only disordered and unsystematic but also are mutually conflicting. All such points obviously make it difficult to know as to what exactly is the view/stand held by the Cārvākas/ Lokāyatikas as a matter of fact.

But even then (as already indicated before), there are number of attempts in modern times which try to carve out the standpoint of Cārvāka from philosophical angle and, in this connection, the philosophy of Cārvāka has been formulated with the coinage of diverse philosophical 'isms'. In the field of epistemology also, it is held that the Cārvāka standpoint adopts some sort of radical empiricism or sensationalism.[1] Mostly, it is held that the Cārvāka philosophy adheres to the stand that crude ordinary sense-perception is the only source of knowledge and it is claimed that it is certain, while all other means are said to be uncertain.

Before making any assessment on this generally approved version of the Cārvāka point of view, it would not be, perhaps, redundant to refer to some obstacles in presenting the Cārvākian position as epistemologically sustainable. The references that are traced as pointing to the Cārvākian thought do not clearly pose the philosophical issues concerning knowledge. There is no evidence of analysis of the concept: knowledge. The subtle distinction between knowledge and knowledge-claim has not been drawn out. No trace of the distinction between 'knowing how' and 'knowing that' is noticed. The distinction between intrinsic validity and extrinsic validity concerning knowledge has neither been referred to nor is critically assessed. There is neither any reference nor any evaluation concerning the distinction between real and true knowledge (*paramārtha/sat jñāna*) and conventional or customary knowledge (*vyāvahārika jñāna*) which is quite notable in the classical Indian philosophical context. There is no exploration of the concept of knowledge with reference to its actual use and application. All these factors lead one to raise doubt as to whether the Cārvāka trend of thought (in whatever way it is noticed at present from various sources) has a distinct clear-cut view in epistemology and also whether the logical implication of the Cārvākian trend of thought

1. D.R. Shastri : *A Short History of Indian Materialism, Hedonism and Sensationalism,* Calcutta: 1957.

points to or support any form of philosophical analysis on such epistemic issues, as it is often advanced in some philosophical circles.

Conceding that there are some such genuine preliminary difficulties, it is not completely futile to move for a fresh philosophical study and appraisal of the Cārvākian trend of thought (in whatever disorderly and distorted form it is available now). As I have already pointed out, a philosophical reading of certain trend of thought is meant for exploring certain new avenue, if it is noticed to be offering a better coherent and consistent picture of the trend. The reading is explorative from a logical perspective, without being just confined to mere literal or etymological description/rendering. The logical basis of the thought is what actually matters for clear understanding and, in that way; to bring forth or to focus on the logical deduction of the original cited expression of the thought does not seem to be an insurmountable task. It is, I think, quite significant and illuminating.

III. The Cārvāka Stand

First of all, it may be noted that the Cārvāka position is: whatever is knowable is empirical. And, the Cārvāka stand is negative about the trans-empirical entity like heaven, hell, soul etc. on account of those being unknowable empirically. That means, knowledge is plausible only insofar as it is empirical. It is only the psycho-physical normal living person who claims for knowledge (whether successful or not). Basically, therefore, any claim of knowledge is primarily sense-bound. In that way, sense-perception is accepted as means/source of knowledge. Here the term 'means' need not be construed as the psycho-physiological process through which knowledge is attained. It implies that sense-perception is the logical ground/reason (*hetu)* for claiming anything as knowledge.

Since the supposition of soul etc. does not satisfy this logical condition that is put outside the periphery of knowledge. In this manner, the Cārvākian assertion that sense-perception (*pratyakṣa*) is the primary mode of rational justification (*pramāṇa*) for claiming knowledge has been advanced. It is argued, in this connection, that the Cārvākian stand not only asserts sense-perception as the primary ground for knowledge, but it also holds that perceptual knowledge is certain whereas the so called knowledge derived from inference etc. is uncertain. But, the opponent of Cārvāka points out that the perceptual knowledge is also not certain. There are ample instances of error like illusory and hallucinatory perception. Perhaps taking a clue from this line of argument, some have moved on to remark that all human knowledge, whether perceptual or non-perceptual are liable to be corrigible and non-sacrosanct. So, ultimately, knowledge in the sense of being absolutely certain is nothing more than a myth. Thus a skeptical conclusion is advanced regarding the validity of all modes of justification and, as such, doubt is raised about the possibility of knowledge itself (cf. Jayarāsi and Nāgārjuna). The idealists like the Vedāntins and others move in a different direction and hold that knowledge in the perfect sense is only attained through direct realization or intuition and all empirical/intellectual-cum-rational knowledge is bound to be imperfect and so is not knowledge proper.

So far as the Cārvākian stand is taken into account, it can be seen that the criterion of certainty in respect of knowledge is never fully withdrawn. It does confirm to the ordinary commonsensical claim that knowledge must be certain, in the sense that one cannot maintain that he knows P and yet P is not. This verbal implication of certainty in respect of knowledge is never challenged. But, at the same time, it does not necessarily follow that whatever one claims to know must be certain or correct. Knowledge-claim is not necessarily knowledge (though it may turn out to be so on very many occasions). And, again it is also notable that what one finds to be certain on some occasion for any purpose, becomes open for change and rectification at a different state later. In this way, the mark of probability is not completely ruled out from anything that is passed as knowledge on one occasion on the basis of the then available data. The Cārvākian stand is logically not committed to rule out this possibility. At the same time, its asserting the primacy of perceptual knowledge and holding it to be certain for all practical purposes seems to be quite legitimate on following ground. It points to the significant empirical fact that the erroneous perception is known to be erroneous by means of another perception only. Hence the primacy of perceptual ground is not affected. The empiric status of knowledge is well retained. It may be argued that even in scientific investigation many discoveries are made possible not through direct/simple sense-perception but through certain complex, sophisticated, technical apparatus/procedure/tools. Sense-perception is not the only factor that is taken into account in various forms of investigation and experimentation. True, this point is quite valid. But it need not be construed that this affects the Cārvāka stand adversely. For, it can be well noted that any theorization and even sophisticated forms of arriving at certain findings do have the logical dependence on the empirical confirmation, either by means of verification or by means of falsification. Granting that conjectures are required for scientific enquiry, it has to be accepted that further critical assessment is necessary for such conjectures. Those are not simply accepted as such. Those require analytical dissection, either to be accepted or to be refuted. And, in this context, empirical methodology obviously works like a remote controller. The documentary source relating to the Cārvāka philosophy does not however spell out all such moves clearly. But that does not matter. The moves are found to be implied from the Cārvākian philosophical stand. On what ground, it may be asked, does a Cārvāka hold that water, air, earth and fire are primary elements? The assertion that all the four elements are primary or basic is not known through sense-perception, but by something more. It is not simply by sense-awareness but by means of some form of non-observational reflective estimation. And if this is the case then, the Cārvākian claim that knowledge is through sense-involvement turns out to be shaky. Further, the opponents point out, in this context, that to accept the four elements as primary or fundamental virtually amounts to the acceptance of supra-sensuous, trans-empirical plane that the four elements are ultimately real (in the metaphysical sense).

There is no literal/textual evidence to trace any counter from the Cārvākian side on such objection but, from logical point of view, the saying that the four elements are primary need not imply that there is the necessary involvement of trans-empirical speculation of the metaphysical transcendence. Even, within the realm of sense the distinction between primary and non-primary is not unwarranted. It is observed that the physical body being old is gradually deteriorated and finally it is seen to have turned into ashes/dusts. The breathing of the living body stops and it is merged with air; the liquid substance turns into water and so on. Hence, to hold that earth, water etc. are primary is virtually grounded on some form of generalization, not completely uprooted from the realm of empirical phenomena. At most, it can be said that in the empirical realm, the sense-mechanism does play its legitimate role, being accompanied by some form of reason that has its operation within the empiric framework alone.

IV. Perception and Sensationalism

It may be noted that the Cārvākian account of perceptual knowledge does not necessarily point to one specific, narrow variety of empiricist doctrine, i.e. sensationalism. The stand that knowledge is due to sense-perception does not imply that the perceptual object is nothing but congeries of sense-impressions or sense-data. The Cārvāka position admits the ordinary objects like land, river, mountain, man, animal, insect as contents of perceptual knowledge. They are viewed as objects of knowledge. This implies that the Cārvāka standpoint does not reduce perceptual knowledge to mere sense-contents; though it very much admits the positive role of sense-involvement in the process of knowing. The ordinary objects of knowledge in the empirical plane like land, river, etc. are possible only when some construction, selection and grouping are formed over and above the sense-data. Ordinary objects of sense-perception are nothing but the outcome of the combined effort of the two factors. And, acknowledging the role of construction in respect of empirical knowledge is never considered as something contrary to its empirical nature itself. Through discrete, fleeting sense-impressions alone the object of empirical knowledge is not accounted. The Cārvāka account of knowledge seems to be well-suited to this rendering than to view it as propounding a doctrine of sensationalism. The object of knowledge is thus one rational construct within the empirical framework. Such a review of the Cārvākian standpoint seems to have confirmation when one finds that some later Cārvākas like Purandara openly declare the validity of inferential knowledge in addition to perceptual knowledge. In case of inference, there is a leap from what is directly observed to something that is not directly observed / sensed (though it is in principle perceptible) and is therefore legitimately inferred. Of course, by admitting inference, the refined Cārvākas never present themselves to be incoherent or inconsistent. They very well establish the point that inferential object of knowledge is not trans-empirical but empirical; and in being empirical it need not warrant of its being directly sense-perceived. Of course, probability (as already hinted) is applicable to both the two types of empirical knowledge (not in the pejorative sense).

By conceding to the point that empirical knowledge aims at objective constructs, the Cārvāka stand does not imply that constructs are substantive entities, having some sort of trans-empirical metaphysical significance. Empirical knowledge primarily rests upon what is presented and over which the construction, as required, is advanced. Sense-presentation is just limited to what occurs in the sense-field. From that any supposition as to what is the origin or source of such presentation and what is the nature of that original source and its scope clearly seems to be one unwarranted an illegitimate expectation (within the Cārvākian logical framework). Such trans-empirical suppositions are ruled out in its philosophy on the ground that there is no rational basis in support of that. To draw the conclusion that Cārvāka's emphasis on the four elements as basic on the ground of their being sense-perceived is bound to point their real nature in the trans-empirical ontological sense seems to be clearly unjustified. The Cārvākian stand is committed to limit its knowledge-claim to the realm of occurrence/appearance and it never moves beyond that. In that way, its account of empirical knowledge is not static but dynamic and is open-textured. It appears that the opponents' insistence on metaphysical foundation for the Cārvākian stand is on account of their own pre-set speculative affiliation, instead of comprehending the rational force of the Cārvākian point of view.

V. The Sources of Knowledge

Despite the remarks from the opponent's sources about the inadmissibility of any source of knowledge, other than perception in the Cārvāka philosophy, reference from the classical source (as already indicated) reveal that Cārvākas admit inference (*anumāna*) in addition to perception. The primacy of perceptual knowledge does not put any obstacle for admitting inference within the empirical sphere. Knowledge derived from both the sources is accepted to be valid, excluding exceptions caused due to certain external factors. *śabda* or *śruti* in the sense of verbal testimony of the scriptures (specially the Vedic source) is obviously ruled out in providing knowledge from the Cārvākian standpoint. Blind acceptance of anything on the basis of dogma, hearsay, prejudiced belief/faith is not possible within the Cārvākian framework. In this manner, the saying "Scriptural testimony is unjustified" (*śabda apramāṇaṁ*) is quite plausible.

But there is another distinct meaning given to *śabda/śruti* in the Indian philosophical context. According to that, *śabda* does not stand for scriptural testimony (Vedic or otherwise). It is defined as verbal/ sentential knowledge through the use and application of sentence/ expression itself.[2] That means, the knowledge derived from *śabda* (*śābdika jñāna*) is verbal knowledge different from factual knowledge. Such knowledge is not derived from senses, but at the same time it is not trans-empirical. For it is very much concerned with empirical state-of-affairs. Verbal knowledge is very much required in the empirical plane and, therefore, its role cannot be gainsaid. From the Cārvākian point of view, such account of *śabda pramāṇa* (linguistic method of justification of verbal knowledge) seems to be not at all inadmissible.[3] The validity of such knowledge can be well accounted therein. It is significant to note that detailed discussion about knowledge and its method of justification is found in the classical Indian philosophical systems. But, there is no reference about any such discussion concerning knowledge neither in the available sources, attributed to Cārvāka nor in the opponent's account of the Cārvākian stand. Even then, at the face of reviewing the philosophy of Cārvāka, such issues can be reflected upon. It is evident that a Cārvāka gives sole emphasis on empirical knowledge. There is absolutely no scope for trans-empirical, transcendental knowledge.

The role of intuition as direct awareness/ realization has obviously no room in the Cārvākian framework. Hence, the classification of knowledge into ultimately perfect type and relatively workable type does not arise at all for a Cārvāka. The distinction between intrinsic and extrinsic validity (*svataḥ* and *parataḥ prāmāṇya*) of knowledge is discussed in detail in some classical sources. Particularly with regard to the Vedic source, the Vedāntins in general subscribe to the doctrine of intrinsic validity. It is pleaded

2. Vācaspati : *Tattvakaumudī* (commentary on *Śāṅkhyakārikā*) *"ṣrutiḥ - vākyajanitam vākyārtha jñānam."*
3. B. Kar : *"śabda-pramāṇa* from the Cārvāka point of view" in Perspectives in Contemporary Philosophy, D. Chakravarty (ed.), Delhi: Ajanta Books International, 1998.

that the knowledge derived from the Vedic utterances is self-valid and does not require any extraneous justification. Obviously, such a position is not accommodated in the Cārvākian philosophy which is committed not to accept anything as valid, if not based on reason.

With regard to the doctrine of extrinsic validity of knowledge, the philosophers, opting for a realistic position in epistemology mostly adopt the stand that validity or justification is dependent on the object, claimed in the knowledge than on the agent or the claimant of the knowledge. So far as the Cārvākian philosophical stand is taken into consideration, it can be pointed out that the issue of knowledge being self-valid can be significant only at the linguistic or verbal label. That means, knowledge as such can never be false. So it is only true by definition. But the assertion "A knows P" or "I know P" are instances of knowledge-claim and that is open for either being true or false. That means, its validity (in the sense of being true) does not depend upon the person's claim but on the objective referent on which the knowledge-claim is made. In that way, the Śaṅkarite stand that knowledge is not agent (knower) dependent *(puruṣavyāpāra-tantra)* but object-dependent (*vastutantra*) is quite significant. The Cārvāka standpoint, it seems, does not have any difficulty in accommodating extrinsic validity of knowledge within its empiric framework; though it cannot support the intrinsic validity of any empirical knowledge-claim.

VI. An observation

Indications have been given before about some conceptual distinction between various uses of knowledge in the working of language. All such subtleties in the use of language are noticed by means of logico-linguistic analysis of the relevant concepts. This, no doubt, contributes to clarity and illumination. Obviously the sources that are attributed to Cārvāka do not contain any such reference. But, as it is mentioned earlier, the philosophical standpoint of Cārvāka has never been detailed out in such sources. So, naturally it is too much to expect in Cārvāka modern philosophical nuances, noticed in the analytical study of the concepts in the concrete setting of the linguistic communication. But, nevertheless, it also needs to be observed that the philosophical stand of Cārvāka, as reviewed here, is clearly prone to treat the concept of knowledge in the empirical plane of concrete setting. It has neither any scope for trans-empirical/metaphysical speculation nor any room for visionary/mystical rendering. Knowledge, as operated in various uses (both in ordinary and technical plane) never demands that. So any subtle distinction that is brought to focus something significant in the use and application of the concept of knowledge in empirical plane is, to be logically precise, not incompatible with the Cārvākian philosophical framework, even though it has never been spelt out in the documentary sources, available till date.

CĀRVĀKA AND MATERIALISM

I. Background

In the modern writings on Cārvāka *darśana*, there is almost full unanimity in identifying it as a materialist philosophy. Such a characterization of the Cārvāka point of view is found to have been firmly established in the scholarly/intellectual circle. Even though one does not come across any direct equivalent term for materialism in the original classical philosophical sources, a term (*bhautikavāda*) has been introduced and, accordingly, the rendering of Cārvāka *darśana* as materialism has got currency. Not only materialism, other established philosophical terms pointing to different 'isms' are also later on incorporated in certain modern accounts of Cārvāka, though with lesser emphasis. The Cārvāka philosophy has been described as 'undisguised materialism', 'crass materialism'[1] and so on.

The reason for identifying it as materialistic is principally as follows. It has accepted four material elements (like earth, *etc.*) as basic constituents of the entire universe. The basic elements are atomistic insofar as those are irreducible to anything else. Consciousness or subjectivity is never regarded as something distinct and independent; but it is derivative out of the typical combination of the four basic elements. At the death of any living being the earthly element relapses into earth and so also the other elements to other basic constituents without anything left as remainder. Since the four irreducible elements are the basic constituents of all that is there, the materialism of Cārvāka is held to be 'a pluralistic atomism'.

---

1. Prasad, Shiv Nath : *op.cit.*, pp. 30-35.

II. Philosophy and Metaphysics

In the classical philosophical literature there is, of course, the presence of materialism, spiritualism, pluralism, monism, idealism, realism, material atomism, mental atomism (monadism) and so on. However, it is notable that all such 'isms' are based on some form of metaphysical presupposition/speculation/stipulation. It is taken for granted that any philosophical position is bound to have metaphysical foundation. Since the philosophical problems center on certain general and universal issues in the abstract plane, it cannot pursue its program of enquiry without making initial/primitive presupposition. It is further pleaded, in this context, that even in other non-philosophical disciplines like sciences and other social sciences, certain basic assumptions or conjectures are accepted as the starting point.

However, in such cases, the assumption is usually specific oriented, being confined to the nature and status of the concerned discipline; whereas in classical philosophy the issues raised are of abstract nature, seeking all-pervasive explanation of its wholeness or totality. For instance, materialism, in that sense, stands for *a priori* assumption that matter alone is real in the all-encompassing sense of universality. Similarly, spiritualism stands for the sole real existence of spirit. Likewise, both monism and pluralism mean either one entity alone is real or many entities are real. In this way, atomism (whether material or spiritual) is a metaphysical standpoint. While metaphysical idealism is idea-centric, metaphysical realism is object-centric. To the former, ideas are only real and to the latter objects are only real. Both the alternatives may either adopt monism or pluralism to suit their own particular views. None of them is bound by any phenomenal limit.

In other words, philosophical theories on the basis of metaphysical speculation turn out to be transcendental to scientific hypothesis. That means, conjectures in different sciences are other than the assumptions made in metaphysics-bound philosophy. While conjectures made in sciences are meant to account various issues in the empirical framework, the assumptions made in metaphysics are speculative in the trans-empirical/transcendental sense. Without the noumenal basis, the metaphysical speculations are just not possible. In certain cases, such speculations are held for explaining the life-world within the empiric frame. But it is to be conceded, in all fairness, that such explanations are more abstract and visionary than having any practical value or sense of workability in the concrete set up.

For instance, the Vedāntins' emphasis on the significance of the ultimate reality of Brahman does not preclude (as quite often it is advanced as a defence) the empirical reality of the world-phenomena is least logically convincing. Because the very sense of ascribing ultimate reality serves as the final goal and the provisional concession to the empiric life-world turns out to be a dwindling patch-work. Similar remark can possibly be made in an altogether different set up, i.e. with respect to Bradley's distinction between appearance and reality.

III. Philosophy and Cārvāka

Despite the scanty source-materials available on Cārvāka, it is encouraging that a philosophical perspective has clear indication in it and that has drawn attention of the traditional as well as modern Indian philosophers, besides some foreigners. The Cārvāka point of view has, of course, the distinction of being an independent and distinct *darśana*, viz, Lokāyata (*lokeṣu-āyata*, meaning thereby aspiration for the welfare/well-being of people at large). However, there are number of opponent sources which mostly condemn, ridicule and vilify the Cārvākas, instead of advancing any rationally convincing arguments/criticisms. In modern expositions of Cārvāka (inclusive of sympathetic writers) there is almost unanimity in depicting Cārvāka as materialist. It is, as already indicated, pleaded that the Cārvāka *darśana* admits four basic elements as irreducibly ultimate real. And, on the ground of admitting the ultimate reality of the material elements alone, the philosophy of Cārvāka can be nothing but materialism. Further, on account of their denial of soul-spirit, God etc., they are clearly anti-spiritualists and, that being so, there is no incongruence, it is argued, in designating their *darśana* as materialism.

Let us have a pause. It is true that minimum data that are available from the original source vindicate that the Cārvāka point of view admits the four elements as basic. But an obvious question can be raised in this context. On what ground, does a Cārvāka admit the four elements as basic? Is it by *a priori* presupposition? Is it because of any prefixed dogma or prejudice? As rationalists (*haitukas*), a Cārvāka is not dogmatically rigid on this issue. He holds that there is the clear sense-perceptual evidence that different things found in nature are primarily of four distinct types and those are found to have been relapsed to the four elements, i.e. earth, water, fire and air. The classification of elements into four basic ones is itself not directly sense-perceived; but definitely it is the outcome of the sense-perceptual source. Any other element is not accepted as basic on the ground of its being not so perceived. In other words, the primacy of four elements is on the basis of perceptibility (knowableness) and not due to any preset *a priori* assumption or metaphysical stipulation. Whether by limiting all human knowledge to perception, the Cārvāka stand is on solid epistemological ground or not is another issue which can be discussed separately. But one thing is clear that the very acceptance of four basic elements is grounded on knowableness of objects and not otherwise. It is not that the metaphysical reality of material elements is first pre-assumed ontologically in the ultimate sense and perception as the method of justification of knowledge comes later to confirm that.

The independent *a priori* existence of the four basic elements as material objects is never the point of contention so far as the logical status of the Cārvāka stand is concerned. In fact, both the issues of existence of any object and its non-existence can be validly raised within the field of knowledge or those are, precisely speaking, epistemic bound. The very admittance of known (*jñeya*) as well as knower (*jñātā*) becomes significant only in the knowledge-situation and the Cārvāka stand seems to be fully in tune with this logical demand. This is fully consistent with its objecting to any form of trans-empirical/transcendental metaphysical existence.

But here a point needs clarification. What is then the nature and status of the four basic elements? Even if it is conceded that they are in principle empirically knowable, do they not exist as natural material objects? Then, what is about there existential status? So far as the Cārvākian standpoint is considered, the existential status of the empirical objects is never questioned. It does not matter whether such objects are sense-perceived actually by a particular person or not. But, side by side it is also to be marked that a Cārvāka is not logically committed to raise the issue, concerning the existence or anything if it is in principle beyond the range of knowableness. The objects in nature and being identified as belonging to material classification are not disputed from the Cārvāka point of view. However, from this it does not imply that the Cārvāka opts for natural classification. The logic of his stand points to the analytical insight that there are no natural classes. It is rather a workable as well as meaningful construction grounded on empirical data. The empiricality of object is not denied.

But from this account, the philosophy of Cārvāka does not embrace the metaphysics of materialism which stands for the ultimate reality of matter as such and nothing else. This, at least, does not follow from his stand, unless somebody is out to graft or superimpose transcendent metaphysics on the Cārvāka stand. But such grafting seems to be an illogical extraneous move. Objects of sense-perception include not only raw objects in natural surrounding but also fine objects which occur due to some form of action/movement of living beings. In such cases, it is not the substantive existent entity (not necessarily material or even physical) but occurred event or movement. The movements noticed in the living beings may be physiological, instinctive and also mental. For a Cārvāka, to recognize mind and its various activities is not a problem. Only his stand is opposed to the admittance of mind as an independent metaphysical transcendent entity. But he is not opposed to mental/ physiological occurrences as empirical phenomena. So also, material objectivity can be accounted in terms of empirical framework without any transcendent metaphysical presupposition of its ultimate reality. The attribution of the concept of matter with metaphysically loaded connotation seems to be unwarranted.

The term '*bhūta*' is meant as matter. In that way the four basic elements, i.e. earth etc. are held as material. And since those elements are said to be basic, the view is held to be materialism. But, the object of knowledge in the Cārvāka stand is not simply material substantive object. It includes living animals and men. The living beings are not passive, inert material objects. Human beings, for example, are conscious being, capable of thinking, feeling and willing. They reveal the sense of choice, freedom, responsibility and other like features which cannot be ascribed to matter as such. So a Cārvāka, admitting object of knowledge in such wide perspective, cannot justifiably be viewed as a materialist. Despite the attribution of the doctrine of epi-phenomenalism, the Carvakian stand cannot logically ignore the subtle as well as significant point of difference between the causal source and the resultant effect.

From the fact of the acceptance of this world (*ihaloka*), it is deduced that his view belongs[2] to materialist philosophy. But this deduction is not that clear and smooth. Because, the support for this world as against other-world is made possible on the basis of empirical knowledge, neither in terms of religious faith nor due to any prejudiced anti-faith attitude. It is not grounded on the

2. *Ibid.*, pp. 146-147.

metaphysical stipulation that matter alone is ultimately real and eternal. The acceptance of material objects and other objects is on the basis of perceptual appearance and not otherwise. The Cārvāka stand does not opt for any closed and finished structure of ultimate reality. Whatever is perceived is not construed to be either unchangeable closed entity or ever changing flux in the sense of metaphysics. The primitive classic concept of matter as static unaltered substantive entity/entities is not acceptable to Cārvāka. The modern scientific concept of 'atom' (as tiny particles containing enormous amount of energy with one nucleus or central particle and what can be seen under powerful electron microscope)[3] is found to be much different from the classic concept of matter and, accordingly, that does not seem to adversely affect the Cārvāka stand which is on firm epistemological ground like that of science.

In this context it seems to be quite significant to formulate a subtle distinction between 'object knowable' and 'object ontologically existing in itself'. 'Object knowable' is, of course, independent of somebody's being actually aware of it. It is conceivable that the planet earth will continue to exist even if all human beings cease to exist as knower. But this also does not necessitate the deduction that earth or any other thing/being would continue to exist/function/occur/ remain eternally or infinitely or timelessly. Such a metaphysical sweep for speculating the object being ultimately existent in the sense of absolute transcendence is what is not logically tenable in the Carvakian framework. Here the critical move, advanced by Cārvāka, is only directed against such visionary/romantic extension of the concept of existence to the noumenal plane, without least questioning the credibility of knowledge in the ordinary commonsensical framework. So objects being there in the natural phenomena are never questioned. In fact the concept of 'natural phenomena' is a legitimate thought-construction on the basis of empirical foundation.

3. *Vide Tell Me Why* (a Reference Book), Octopus Publishing Group Ltd., 2-4 Heron Quays, London E44 JP, 2001-2007, p. 74.

Thus the Cārvākian stand faces no difficulty in admitting the objects as natural and the concept of nature is not to be considered as recalcitrant to its logical tone. But views like 'materialism', 'naturalism' too, as a metaphysically loaded concept (implying nature as one basic substantive entity alone as real existent), seems to be unacceptable in the Cārvākian framework.

IV. Common Sense and Science

The available documentary sources on the Cārvāka stand do not point out any distinction between the commonsensical and scientific claim of knowledge. This is quite obvious in view of the period and other relevant factors in which such sources were composed. But when one is to philosophically analyze the logical foundation of Cārvāka point of view, one need not, it seems, be bound by such omissions (which are otherwise quite important to be pursued). As hinted before, a philosophical exercise of a particular point of view rests upon its rational/logical cogency and viability.

Prima facie, it appears to be clear that the Cārvāka stand is limited to crude commonsense by accepting knowledge in terms of sense-perception. There is no mention about the distinction between direct and indirect knowledge. There is no indication between perception and sensation. Even the vital differences between simple observation and laboratory experiment are not noticed therein. Whatever is sense perceived/perceivable is accepted and beyond empirical domain nothing is admitted. It may sound like "*esse est percipii*"; but it does not move to the extent of embracing either the philosophical theories of idealism or immaterialism.

When one attempts to bring forth the philosophical implications of the Cārvākian stand, one is required to be somewhat cautious and he need not be swept away by some apparent points of similarity. So far as the Cārvāka point of view is concerned, its adherence to the empirical foundation of knowledge is neither committed to accept the metaphysical idealism/immaterialism nor even to accept metaphysical realism/materialism. As a matter of fact, it is not bound to make any move from epistemological front to metaphysical dimension. The materialistic stand that matter alone is real ultimately is not derived from empirical knowledge. It is a metaphysical presupposition and, as such, it is not at all acceptable to the logical foundation of the Cārvāka stand. Precisely speaking, it is far from metaphysical commitment of any 'ism'.

Even in the field of epistemology, accepting the legitimate role of sense-operation, its account of knowledge is not necessarily reduced to either sensory ideas or sense-impressions. It reveals its clear option for the ordinary conception of objective knowledge, free from any ontological commitment. And, in this way, the Cārvāka standpoint need not be rated as a primitive form of crude materialism, to be dumped into the hoary past of antiquity. Its standpoint, being logically articulated and reconstructed, can be found as quite relevant in the modern perspective.

The Cārvākian concept of *bhūta* is very much unlike the traditional philosophical concept of matter as solid, unconscious, passive substance. *Bhūta* is held to be mobile. And, in that way, it is close to the scientific notion of atom which consists of number of tiny particles, having enormous amount of energy and thus is dynamic in nature. It never holds the metaphysical conclusion that atoms are alone real in the sense of being eternal. Like that of science, the Cārvākian stand seems to be on the basis of evidential probability. That safeguards the open-texture feature of the Cārvākian point of view. If traditionally philosophy is inseparably tied up with some form of metaphysical speculative construction, then what can be the prospect of the Cārvākian stand, being free from metaphysical 'ism'? What would then be its philosophical basis?

V. Cārvāka and the Life-world

The logical foundation of the Cārvākian thought does not, as it is seen, move for setting any metaphysical system in the traditional sense. A Cārvāka does neither clearly formulate any distinctly elaborate view about the life-world as some contemporary philosophers advocate, nor does he precisely spelt out that philosophy is not a theory, but an activity as many analytical philosophers maintain. But, definitely some logical implications from the varied and discrete sayings that are attributed to Cārvāka can be drawn out, which are philosophically quite insightful.

A Cārvāka views human life in the natural empiricist setting. People are born to a situation and through care; nourishment of the elders and also the environmental congeniality, the normal human child grows and develops its different conscious activities. He moves towards adapting the diverse circumstances that he faces and develops the sense of sociality to have a cordial relation with other fellow beings, in order to have a happy and peaceful living, minimizing the difficulties that he comes across. A composite outlook is aimed at for sustaining the socio-individual relations, avoiding tension, conflict and discordant elements. Social morality is adhered to on account of practical reasoning, without fully sacrificing the valid individual preferences. There is a justifiable move, often advanced to maintain balance between socio-individual needs and requirements, also taking care of the eco-system as far as possible.

It seems that a Cārvāka is not against this normal expectation. He takes up living in a normal setting. He has not shown any escapist or negative approach to life and, in this way, pleads for a this-worldly outlook. He does not ignore the fact of pain and suffering; but appeals to face those calmly as well as bravely, with a view to overcome those by undertaking suitable means and procedures. And, for that, a rational practical outlook is indicated, without damaging the socio-human moral sense (which would be discussed in detail later on). Hence, though a complete full-fledged, well-articulated specific theory of life-world is not traced in the original sources, ascribed to the Cārvākas, a general viewpoint of Cārvāka on such issues can be formulated afresh with some positive result instead of losing consistency.

Quite legitimately, the Cārvāka point of view is critical about any other-worldly existence of living person as a disembodied soul/ spirit in the trans-empiric metaphysical realm of noumena. Not simply it is empirically unknowable (in principle), but it is also not plausible. Cārvāka does not, of course explicitly makes such declarative assertion. But it seems to be clearly implied from his critical reasoning. That is why his option for the normal living in the natural empiric setting speaks well of his otherwise less articulated view about life-world. His view, in this regard, is not necessarily man-centric in the sense of *homo mensura* (that man is the measure of everything). But his stand seems to be quite open-textured and liberal insofar as the life of man is viewed amidst the natural surroundings, within the empiric setting. It seems, he is not necessarily refractory to have one general sense of weltanscha-uung. Only it is to be empirically rooted without any transcendental anchorage.

VI. Suffering

Pain/suffering is a fact of living. It is an undeniable phenomenon and the Cārvākian standpoint does not ignore this empirical fact. The very admittance of the fact of suffering in living beings amounts to suggest (to Cārvāka) that different modes of living consciousness like knowing, feeling and willing are empirical occurrences, despite the fact that the consciousness is the outcome of the four elements. In other words, the admittance of embodied consciousness clearly affirms the empirical reality of its different modes. And, in that way, there is no incongruence in accepting its empiricality. Everybody (inclusive of men and animals) suffers. The Cārvāka stand duly acknowledges that suffering is either physical or mental or both.

The classical Indian philosophers while recognizing the problem of suffering offer different solutions to face the problem and to redress it. For instance, the Buddhists are well-known in proclaiming that everything is intrinsically filled with sorrows and sufferings (*sarvaṁ duḥkhaṁ*). While reflecting over this, they try to locate its ground and then appeal to remove the ground; so that it ceases fully. The Sāṁkhya philosophers refer to the fact of suffering and hold that discriminative knowledge (*vivekī jñāna*) alone can cause cessation of suffering. The Vedāntins, in general, also speak about human suffering due to human being's involved/entangled with worldly attachment (*saṅsāra/moha*). In this context, the performance of detached action/duty (*naiṣkarmya*) of the *Bh. Gītā* is referred to. By attaining the state of complete non-attachment, there results full cessation of suffering and also positive bliss (*mahā sukha/ānanda*).

The Cārvākas, in this regard, have clear reference to happiness (*sukha*) while living, especially in and through human existence. Obviously, happiness is desired at the background of meeting effectively the challenge of suffering. Since suffering is an empirical fact, there is no point in ignoring that. It has to be faced. The ways and means have to be explored to meet the challenge within the empirical framework. This is, of course, one existential issue and solution at the practical front is of bare necessity. A Cārvāka never disowns the responsibility, particularly when it is of a grave human concern.

However, the effort for redressing suffering never suggests that there is, as a matter of fact, an ultimate state of living in which there is full cessation of suffering. Even the socalled enlightened person (*jīvan-mukta*) cannot be conceived as fully sense-opaque and, as such, is exposed to both pain and pleasure. The practical message, in this context, is rather to minimize suffering as far as practicable. And, likewise the effort is to attain happiness as far as possible. Neither there is the presence of full suffering nor full happiness in human existence. So the Cārvākian stand of desiring happiness needs to be understood in this contextual background.

This shows that a Cārvāka is not for any mythical ideal of complete happiness/bliss. It is not because of its peculiar temperament or attitude or personal preference. It is because such a mythical state is groundless. Its existence is not prone to reason. There is the clear empirical necessity that a life is born, grown and then extinct. So during this span of existence, there is the admixture of pain and pleasure etc. Man, in his own reasonable effort, requires to get happiness and to avoid sorrows and sufferings as far as practicable. Cārvāka is not for a fresh stipulative definition of the terms: life, existence, and conscious living being (*puruṣa*) in terms of trans-empirical transcendental reality which virtually caters to one's own personal vested interest, mostly due to romanticized emotion and feeling. By recognizing the factuality of pain and pleasure, sorrows and happiness and others (usually categorized as mental occurrences), the Cārvāka stand cannot validly accommodate metaphysics of materialism. The empiricist view of life is clearly independent of materialistic/spiritualistic leanings. It treats life as it is without being otherwise. In fact, the empirical view of life does not seem to have been loaded with the implication of any transcendent metaphysics.

VII. Observation

Critical remark on metaphysics is not new. It has been raised in the philosophical circle long since (both in east and west). The Cārvākas have raised their voice against trans-empirical metaphysical speculations. Jayarāsi has pointed put the futility of all methods of justification (*pramāṇas*) for the establishment of metaphysical concept (*tattva*). So also, Nāgārjuna has become critical about all valid modes of categorization (*catuṣkoṭi*) for the comprehension of ultimate reality and thus has concluded his philosophical reflection only on non-commitment (*śūnyatā*), without giving any scope for metaphysical costruction.[4] All these approaches are precisely against all forms of metaphysical constructions of any form of essentialism.

4. Nayak, G.C. : *Mādhyamika Śūnyatā,* ICPR, New Delhi, 2001.

Bacon is, perhaps, the first bold thinker in west to raise voice against all *idolas* in his New Method (*Novum Organum*) which seems to have an indirect adverse impact on the metaphysical construction. The empiricist program of limiting human knowledge to sense-experience has taken a radical turn in Hume's empiricism and his attack on metaphysics ('commit it to flames') is quite well known. Kant's *Prolegomena to any future metaphysics* and his insightful pointing to antinomies on the exclusive employment of ideas of reason are note worthy. In the modern times, attack on metaphysics has become conspicuous in positivism (Comte), logical positivism (Vienna Circle), and logical empiricism (Ayer). Philosophical analysts, under the leadership of Wittgenstein, are found to be somewhat hesitant to make such move against metaphysics like the logical positivists and empiricists; but nevertheless they are also found to be critical about metaphysical speculative construction, though in a softer tone. In this context, Wittgenstein's remark that whereof one cannot speak, one must consign to silence (*Tractatus*), Neurath's comment on it 'One must indeed be silent, but not about anything' and Ramsey's rejoinder that one cannot whistle it either are notable. Wittgenstein's later analytical writing is also found to be critical about metaphysical essentialism (*Investigation*).

Philosophers have in recent past started to review metaphysics again amidst all such critical reflections. Some feel that such attacks by the critic only reveal that metaphysics is only extruded not exploded (Hampshire). Attempts are made to classify metaphysics into two broad types: descriptive and revisionary (Strawson), indicating thereby preference for the former than the latter. Some again have become critical about the non-metaphysical drive, made by the positivists/empiricists as well as philosophical analysts and have shown their preference for a revival of metaphysics, of course, in a strikingly different sense (existentialists and phenomenologists). Discussion on such movements in respect of metaphysics would be taken later. Bradley's remark "The anti-metaphysician is a brother metaphysician with a rival theory of his own" is quite often referred to in this connection.

Amidst all these moves noticed in philosophical circle, it is interesting to reflect over the Cārvākian stand in order to properly assess and evaluate its relevance at present. It can be seen that the Cārvākian stand is only against speculation of trans-empirical/ transcendent metaphysics. Its criticism is primarily based on the epistemic ground which is limited to the empirical jurisdiction. The world-phenomena/life-world/natural order is acceptable to a Cārvāka not on the ground of its being directly sense-perceived. The life-view of the Cārvāka stand is definitely not the outcome of sense-perception. But, even then, the Cārvākian life-world is constructed only on the basis of empirical foundation. Such move is entertained only insofar as it is found to be proper enough to give a reasonably workable account of the empirical knowledge as a whole. It is not simply because of the inaccessibility of trans-empirical knowledge, the Cārvāka stands for the empirical theory of knowledge; but on the logical ground, it holds that any trans-empirical claim of knowledge ultimately needs its confirmation in the empirical source and not reversely.

The rise and development in different formal systems cannot be ignored. In such cases, the arriving at a theoretical conclusion is dependent on internal consistency and logically approved deduction, without expecting any empirical confirmation. All this need not be opposed to the Cārvāka stand. But, it is not irrelevant to point out, in this regard, that the general overall acceptance of a formal system is just not limited to its formal or abstract coherency/consistency. Either directly or indirectly, it has to be shown as to how the formal system is to be applied and worked out at the concrete plane. The applicative and operational significance of the formal system is of bare necessity which is introduced either immediately or in a remote complex procedure. But, nonetheless, the applicative move is logically warranted and on the basis of that the strength of the formal system rests.

If this line of reflection has some sense of relevancy, then the Cārvāka standpoint need not be brushed aside. It does have a point to be taken up seriously. From the logical foundation of the Cārvākian philosophical stand, it can be seen that it is not necessarily opposed to consider such conjecture/hypothesis that is directed to account the empirical knowledge as more reasonably strengthened. And, if such conjecture amounts to the admittance of some type of empiricist-bound metaphysics, clearly ignoring all transcendent visionary surmises, then the Cārvāka stand seems to have no reluctance against that. That would not then be "a rival theory of the anti-metaphysician." It would, on the contrary, be on the bedrock of common sense as well as science. Science as "organized common-sense" (Cunningham) is posed as an improvement on ordinary common sense, not a total rejection of it.[5]

---

5. In my earlier writing, I have not questioned in detail the materialistic rendering of Cārvāka. Vide my "Ethics in Classical Indian Materialistic Philosophy" in *A Historical Developmental Study of Classical Indian Philosophy of Morals* (*ed.* Prof. Rajendra Prasad), published by PHISPC, Centre for Studies in Civilization, New Delhi-110019, 2009.

CĀRVĀKA AND ATHEISM

I. Nāstika

The Sanskrit word *nāstika* is usually meant as an atheist (disbeliever in the existence of God[1] or a denier of the Vedic authority.[2]). Though both the meanings are not identical in the classical Indian writings, they are often found to have been used interchangeably. Acceptance or denial of the Vedic scriptural authority has primarily a religio-theological root and accordingly both Bauddha and Jaina *dharma* (as religion) are opposed to the Vaidika dharma. But, it is also noticed that while the Pūrva and Uttara Mīmāṁsā philosophers (*darśanajñas*) adhere to the Vedic root on their respective mode of justification, the Sāṅkhya-Yoga and the Nyāya-Vaiśeṣika philosophers clearly opt for independent philosophical justification of their respective standpoints, without depending upon the Vedic authority. Even some of them have been found as overtly critical about any pre-acceptance of the Vedic source. At the same time, it is also notable that they do not move to the extent of either embracing the Bauddha and Jaina philosophies or their religious facets.

The Cārvāka point of view, it can be seen, neither on philosophical nor on religious basis accepts the Vedic alliance. The Cārvāka standpoint is distinctly philosophical that is conceded even in tradition - (*Vide* Mādhavācārya's *Sarva Darśana Saṅgraha*)

1. Fowler, F.G and Fowler, H.W. (compiled), *The Pocket Oxford Dictionary*, Oxford: Clarendon Press, 1955 reprint, p. 42.
2. Apte, V.S., *The Student's Sanskrit-English Dictionary*, Delhi: New Bharatiya Book Corporation, 2000, p. 285 (on the authority of *Śiśupālabadha* and *Manusmṛti*).

without having any religious affinity. All this suggests that the primacy of the acceptance of the Vedic authority lies on religious ground and whatever philosophical justifications are advanced in certain quarters; those are mostly aimed at to support the religious clinging in some way or other. As regards the other meaning, disbelief in the existence of God (or Supreme Being as creator of the universe) is found to have been used extensively in common popular level.

Both the Bauddha and the Jaina *dharmas* are treated as *nāstika dharma* in the sense of disbelieving any God or Supreme Being as creator. But, on philosophical ground, at least in certain cases both Buddhism and Jainism have been found as not justifying either belief or disbelief of such transcendental Being or God. Such philosophical sense of transcending the issue of God is more conspicuous in the Sāṅkhya-Yoga (particularly in its early formulation), where the concept of God (*Īśvara*) is exposed as unjustifiable (*asiddha*) and such a concept can at best be designated as special *puruṣa* (*puruṣa viśeṣa- Yoga-sūtra*) but never as a creator (God) in the theistic sense. The *tattvas* (philosophically accepted as primary concepts), admitted in the philosophy of Sāṅkhya-Yoga are distinctly non-theistic. Similar thing is noticed in the Nyāya-Vaiśeṣika admittance of different *tattvas*. There is no mention of *Īśvara* therein, despite the attempt made by some later Naiyāyikas to introduce *Īśvara* within their philosophic framework. But it is also noticed that such inclusion is not logically warranted to the Nyāya-Vaiśeṣika philosophical stand and it only caters to the need of some extra-philosophical purpose. Similar is the case with the Cārvākas. Their admittance of four basic elements as *tattvas* does not mean basic realities in the supra-empirical metaphysical sense; but only basic concepts in their philosophical framework.[3]

The Cārvākas, as hinted before, have neither found any justification for the acceptance of the Vedic orthodoxy nor for the

---

3. Warder, A.K., *A Course in Indian Philosophy*, 2nd edn. Delhi: MLBD, 1998, p. 122.

admittance of a theological Supreme Being or God (*Īśvara*). That amounts to suggest (according to the prevailed view) that the Cārvāka philosophers are *nāstikas* in both the senses. Here, the issue of atheism in the philosophy of Cārvāka remains obviously the focal point of discussion.

It goes without saying that its philosophy has been given exposition as atheistic by both foreign and Indian scholars/ researchers. It is taken for granted that its philosophy amounts to the disbelief in God. Such a view is mostly grounded on the available Cārvāka sources (as stated by its opponents and the same collected by some writers in anthology and compendium). Since the Cārvākas, it is held, are critical about the admittance of any form of supernaturalism (that transgresses sense-empiricism), the belief in God or theistic Supreme Being as creator is supposed to have been ruled out as the only legitimate consequence. And, further, the cancellation of belief amounts to, it is presumed, the point that disbelief remains as the only alternative which the philosophy of Cārvāka is bound to honour.

II. Belief and Knowledge

Let there be a pause to review the whole matter. First of all, let it be noted that the issue concerning either belief or disbelief in God is not same as believing or disbelieving anything/event pertaining to the empirical framework. The issue is, as said earlier, something concerning trans-empirical realm. Not only that. It is further implied that the belief in such a trans-empirical/supra-sensuous being is advocated at the religio-theological background. The Semitic religion stands for a belief in a supernatural Power/Being to whom one is to obey/worship and surrender out of utter belief/faith. In other words, here belief is distinctly faith-oriented and, as such, it becomes a matter of personal attitude and preference, partly based on concerned group or community's persuasive appeal and propaganda. All this is backed by some form of emotion.

So far as the logical implication of the Cārvāka philosophic standpoint is concerned, it should be born in mind that it never advances sheer *a priori* speculation about knowledge in its conceptual framework. It starts with the commonsense setting of knowledge. It does not advocate sense-empiricism of the variety of bare sensationalism. The ordinary object of knowledge is not, according to its stand, is not just impressions but a meaningful construct on the foundation of sense-impressions. That is why such construct is not construed as absolutely independent *a priori* metaphysical entity, free from empiric data; but can be treated as some sort of empiric construct, required for the formulation of knowledge whatsoever. There is thus neither any explicit nor any implicit indication to have any pre-acceptance of bare metaphysical speculative stand. The Cārvākian stand, I suppose, is set to explicate the logical basis of knowing and, in this regard, it seems to trace out its claim and justification. When it advocates that sense-perception is the most dependable source of knowing, it appears, the point of emphasis is not on any psychological process of human knowing, but only to point out the logical condition of knowing anything in the ordinary normal human setting.[4] It seems to be quite cognizant of the fact that whatever is known by means of sense-perception is at times found to be illusory/erroneous and, as such, one cannot even justifiably claim that knowledge claimed by means of sense-perception is absolutely certain. In other words, if something is known as existing empirically, it is never construed as ultimate and really existent. This is due to the simple ground that sense-perception is operative within the specific setting of phenomena and not otherwise. Therefore, any claim for limitless, absolute, eternal really real existence is not within the jurisdiction of knowledge that is actually in operation. The use of the concept of knowledge in the logico-linguistic set up is very much in tune with its applied occurrence.

4. Here 'knowing' is taken up in a broader way that includes descriptive as well as performative senses.

To put in another way, the sense of ultimate/absolute/most perfect etc. are normally considered as the ideal standard which need not be jumbled up with actuality. The 'ideal' virtually serves as the limiting concept for visionary aspiration and also it may be a boosting factor for further advancement/progress in the operational level on some occasion. In this way, it is likely to be persuasive, encouraging and inspiring. Even such reading of persuasion etc. need not be questioned from the Cārvākian philosophical stand. This step is quite plausible and normally befitting. But, from this to make a sweeping move in the plane of reason that such visionary ideal is ultimately real and it points to existence as such which is far or most superior to the actual existence, turns out to be an illegitimate/unreasonable demand.

True, whatever is found in natural phenomena is never rejected by the Cārvākas. Those are considered as real and existent for all practical purpose. By this acceptance, certain theoretical issues concerning their occurrence and the possibility of being otherwise are, of course, not ruled out. That nature does not necessarily behave uniformly is not simply a theoretical expectation, but it is a matter of fact. The Cārvāka point of view does not dispute about that. But that does not imply that disorder found in natural phenomena is something supernatural. It is noticed empirically and any supernatural (in the sense of transcendental/metaphysical) explanation is not called for. The very fact of abnormal or extra-ordinary happening in natural phenomena requires, of course, an explanation. And, in this regard, any sort of scientific enquiry to trace out its causal and other auxiliary factors is well taken up within the empirical bounds and any trans-empirical speculative surmise is logically not compelling. Rather, it can be noted that the demand for such trans-empirical account rests upon the imaginative conjecture pointing to the suggestion that real existence must be unchangeable ultimate and that can be realized by some form of supra-sensuous, supra-intellectual form of mystic intuition. Such an insistence, from the Cārvākian perspective, is held to be baseless and unwarranted.

III. Theism and Atheism

With this point of explanatory clarification, let the issue concerning the controversy between theism and atheism be probed into from the Cārvākian standpoint. As already indicated, both theism and atheism centre on the issue about belief or disbelief in the existence of God as the Supreme Being. In this sense, the dispute is on existence or non-existence of God.[5] It can be noted that the disputants, in this regard, never raise the point that whether God exists or does not exist as a matter of fact like any other being or thing (in the empirical plane). Because if that would be the case, then that could be very easily settled by available means of normal verification.

It is precisely based on another stipulative meaning of the concept: existence. From this angle, the normal phenomenal public empirical existence of anything or being is not real but apparent. Behind this veil of appearance, the religio-theological demand is that there is the really real form of ultimate existence (not limited by space and time structural frame) and God, as the Supreme Being, fulfils that expectation. He is speculated as omnipresent, omniscient and omnipotent. In this way, He is conceived as the creator, sustainer and destroyer of the entire universe. Though He is thought to be not limited to the empiric level of phenomena, He is also regarded to be immanent in the world-process and there, total exclusive transcendence is not insisted upon in theistic religio-theological framework. In other words, God is said to be both immanent and transcendent. The issue of belief or disbelief (in form of theism or atheism) is raised in this context.

5. In the general theistic framework, there is the admittance of multiple conceptions, i.e. monotheism, polytheism etc. Thus it accommodates one Supreme God and also plural number of gods and goddesses. However, in any case, the sense of trans-empiric, trans-mundane transcendence is all through retained in the religio-theological framework.

The Cārvāka philosophical position is not rooted either on a theistic or on athėistic (anti-theistic) foundation. The question of advocating or decrying religious-cum-theological belief/disbelief does not seem to be the point at issue in its context. The fundamental philosophical issue, with which the Cārvāka stand is concerned, is rather for tracing and analyzing the nature and scope of the legitimate use of the concept of knowledge in the socio-individual plane that happens within the normal setting of empirical phenomena. Sense-perception is, no doubt, admitted by them as most fundamental in this regard. The logical implication of such a stand is not outright rejection of inference etc. But it only suggests that such extra-perceptual means must have its root in and through the empirical mode of cognition. The sense of confirmation of any inferential claim must point to perception in some way or other (either directly or indirectly). To put it differently, the empirical confirmability of knowledge is implied all through.

Conceding this point, the Cārvāka stand raises questions about the theistic notion of knowledge-claim about God's existence which is framed at the background of supra-sensuous/supra-natural transcendence. The Cārvākian point asserts that the use of the concept of knowledge is legitimate within the empirical foundation and, in no way, it can be logically extended to something beyond. So the reasoning which is advanced by theists to justify the knowledge-claim of transcendental existence of God is questioned and is argued to be not valid. The trans-empiric extension of inferential reasoning and even that of scripture (*śruti*) is challenged in this context. This is virtually on the ground of intelligibility and comprehension. Such an extension of the meaning of the concept: knowledge and also that of existence is indicated to be conceptually muddling.

If this point is well taken, then it can be seen that the Cārvākian philosophical stand is not concerned about belief or disbelief about God on the ground of personal attitude/sentiment; but it is oriented to expose the fallacious, invalid mode of reasoning that is advanced by its opponent at the conceptual plane. A question, raised by the

Cārvākas, about the ground for establishing the existence or non-existence of God is found to be somewhat similar to that of logical positivism, as exposed by Ayer[6] in the sense that the Cārvākian form of logical empiricistic stand is distinctly beyond the dispute encircling both theism and atheism.

IV. Agnosticism and Scepticism

The Cārvākian stand is also not agnostic in the sense that it does not assert that there exists some transcendental being/being which is unknown and unknowable. It, on the other hand, holds that such a supposition is logically faulty. The utterance: "God does not exist" amounts to suggest that something described as God does not exist. That would imply that God who is so and so does not exist. But, in that case, the description ascribed to the concept of God is supposed to be self-explanatory which it is virtually not. Because any description ascribed to the concept of God is found to be logically not comprehensible. "God as the perfect being exists" is not literally significant, even though it is said to have, on some occasion, figurative or metaphysical significance. And, it is evident that both theists and anti-theists, accepting such description as significant (literally) move on to react about God's existence either affirmatively or negatively and that is precisely what is not rationally compelling.

The Cārvāka philosophy is not to settle as to what actually exists and what is not. That issue is well determined by the available means and procedure, other than any form of conceptual analysis. It is clear that any type of scientific pursuit takes care of that issue and the Cārvākian stand does not oppose that. Its philosophical probing in terms of conceptual analysis is different from factual investigation. The former is aimed at clarification for the purpose of intelligible comprehension and the latter is for the advancement of knowledge with a view to attain some sort of novel information/skill of factual significance.

6. Ayer, A.J., *Language, Truth and Logic,* Dover Publications, 1953, pp. 115-117.

The Cārvākian stand definitely points to reason (*hetu*) and holds that on rational ground, neither belief nor disbelief about the existence/non-existence of God (that is by definition supra-empirical and super-natural) is called for. Both existence and non-existence are meaningfully used in the empirical plane. But to extend those to supra-empiric noumenal plane of transcendence and, again, claiming that extension as causing knowledge is not reasonable. The Cārvākian/Lokāyatika emphasis on *hetu* is well noted by Kauṭilya in his *Arthaśāstra* where he admits the inclusion of Lokāyata as *darśana* on the basis of its adhering to rational probing (*ānvīkṣikī*) as against sticking to dogmas and prejudices.[7]

It is already hinted that the philosophy of Cārvāka need not be treated as a form of scepticism. It does not raise dispute about the ordinary sense of knowledge that is operated in common sense. And also, it is not antagonistic to scientific pursuit which, being rooted in common sense, moves beyond quite consistently in the same empirical/natural/phenomenal realm to trace out new findings that are beneficial to mankind at large. So, in this sense, its position is not at all sceptical. It does not also cling to any form of agnosticism. No *a priori* presupposition concerning either "substance in itself" or "things in themselves" is entertained by it. In fact, its stand is not to raise any issue (on rational ground) as to what exists in itself (really/ultimately). It, as is evident, remains all through critical about any *a priori* supra-sensuous transcendental metaphysical presupposition. Its philosophy is rather confined to what appears in the phenomenal level and all sorts of conjectures, hypotheses and even presuppositions are meaningfully framed within that legitimate limit. If at all its stand is to be characterized as metaphysical, it can only be, perhaps, termed as "metaphysics of experience" to borrow a phrase, coined by H.J. Paton, of course, in a different context.[8]

7. *"sāṅkhya-yogo lokāyata cetyanvīkṣikī"* - *Arthaśāstra,*102.
8. Paton, H.J., Kant's *Metaphysics of Experience,* London : George Allen & Unwin Ltd., 1951.

True, the Cārvāka philosophy is critical about the theological approach of justifying the theist's claim of the existence of God on rational ground. So also, it is critical about the anti-theist's arguments concerning non-existence of God. It only is directed to show that arguments as well as counter-arguments are sensibly applicable to the sphere of phenomena where significantly the knowledge-claim is advanced and it is also determined either positively or negatively. It seems that the Cārvāka position is logically committed only to emphasize the rational justification of valid knowledge-claim. It does not thereby encroach upon the matters of faith or no-faith which are on non-rational (not irrational) ground, i.e. on the basis of personal attitude or sentiment. May be in some cases, such faith becomes an impetus to generate peace of mind and tranquillity to the concerned person. The Cārvākian stand need not be opposed to that. It raises logical difficulty only when there is an attempt to justify such beliefs or anti-beliefs on par with usual knowledge-claim on rational ground.

In human life, there are very many facets which are not prone to knowledge but to emotional satisfaction like enjoyment of art, music and even following certain moral principles radically, regardless of other practical factors. So long as such non-cognitive pursuits (which are quite important in their respective sphere) do not adversely affect the normal course of socio-human transaction including human welfare at large; those are not discouraged and the Cārvākian stand is not opposed to that. In that sense, it is not crassly indifferent to use and application of moral norms/principles as long as those do not obstruct the smooth course of socio-individual living in the empirical realm. The usual sense of human welfare cannot be sacrificed on that account. The detailed analytical review on the Cārvākian philosophical stand on morality will be discussed later.

Whatever is expressed here with regard to the position of a believer, similar thing is also applicable *mutatis mutandis* to that of a disbeliever (in the common level). Both need not be reasonably touched by the logical analysis implied in the Cārvākian philosophical stand. As a matter of fact, the philosophy of Cārvāka turns out to be a critic of theologism as well as anti-theologism, without touching upon the issue of belief or disbelief at the personal level that need not necessarily demand any rational justification. It is remarked that a Cārvāka neither hates God nor fosters God, but he is indifferent to God who is unseen.[9] Of course, a Cārvāka neither has any ill-will nor any affection towards God or no-God in the supra-empirical sense. But any such assertion concerning transcendental existence or non-existence, according to him, is not set aside simply because of its being unseen; but because it is not cognizable on the ground of reason (*hetu*). So the Cārvākian position seems to be not indifferent in the sense of being just neutral. It need not be viewed as callous or radically unconcerned to such personal religious feeling (that is not necessarily bent upon any theological boosting) insofar as it is not recalcitrant to smooth flow of socio-empiric human living, without unbalancing the general eco-system of natural surroundings. But any attempt of rationally justifying such emotions and sentiments as either equal competitor or even as more superior to general sense of cognitive knowing on the rational plane is definitely questioned from the Cārvākian point of view.

The approach of Cārvāka is not to remain opaque to what happens actually and what is contrary to human interest. Here interest does not rest upon any sort of crude individualism/egotism. Interest signifies, in this context, that which is proper for the humanity in the collaborative strength of socio-individual proper needs and requirements. In this way, the stand seems to be quite congenial for a harmonious balanced reciprocity and adjustment between both social and individual necessities. Of course, for achieving that no transcendental boosting is ever sought forward. The issues are empirical and, therefore, those are to be tackled empirically. So the moral approach to the problem can be legitimately entertained within the empiric sojourn and not beyond that. In this way, genuine

9. Prasad, S.N., *Chārvāka/Lokāyata, op.cit.*, p. 248.

emotion and sentiment that lie in man's personal being may not be impeded; for it does not hinder the peaceful run of human living in general. However, individual cases of difficulty and difference can be settled contextually.

So, on the basis of the present discussion, it seems that the Cārvāka philosophical stand can be meaningfully reviewed and reconstructed, particularly as against the wide-spread view of its being tied up with atheism or anti-theism. The very dichotomous stand between theism and atheism does not operate; for that is not found to be logically exhaustive in this regard. There is a clear scope for opting to a different setup which remains independent on its own footing, without necessarily being clubbed into any one of the two opposites.

CĀRVĀKA AND MORALITY

I. Puruṣārtha

Usually the view-point of the Cārvākas is ridiculed by the opponents as grossly immoral. They are not only censured as atheist (*anīśvaravādī*), hater of the holy scriptures (*Veda nindakaḥ*) and worst sinner (*pāpiṣtha*) but are also condemned as squarely sexual rather sexually pervasive (*kāmāsakta*). They are even decried as socially obnoxious, having no regard to other's legitimate needs and preferences. Thus the position of the Cārvāka is viewed as utterly self-centred, egoistic and individualistic, having least social concern or responsibility. In this way, a Cārvāka is criticized as not only anti-spiritual but as heavily immoral and inhuman. The criticism tends to suggest that the Cārvāka stand and morality are poles asunder.

In the *Brāhaspatya sūtra* (henceforth BS), there is a reference about Cārvāka's supreme preference for sexual indulgence.[1] But, again there is also the reference about both sex and wealth as of supreme value.[2] Obviously, both the cited references cannot be regarded as authentic stand of the Cārvākas. Firstly, both the views are not mutually congruent. The second view states something more and is thus not compatible with the first. Secondly, in both the references, there is the occurrence of *puruṣārtha* - the supreme value or the ultimate goal of human being (*puruṣa*). Either the conception of *trivarga* (i.e., three-fold classification of *dharma, artha* and *kāma*) or the conception of *caturvarga* (i.e., four-fold classification of *dharma, artha, kāma* and *mokṣa*) as the final goal is clearly found to

1. *"Kāma evaikaḥ puruṣārthaḥ"* BS.5.
2. *"Arthakāmau puruṣārtho"* BS.27.

be a later composition in the orthodox (*pāramparika*) scheme of life-view. During the earliest formulation of the Cārvāka/Lokāyata view-point whose references are noticed in the Vedas, there is no mention of the concept of *puruṣārtha*.

The concept generally stands for the meaning/purpose or aim of life. In that sense, it points to the accomplishment of the goal of human life. The orthodox Vedic point of view is mostly regarded to have adopted a scheme of life in tune with the natural surroundings. And, in due course, the splendid natural phenomena, inclusive of water, fire, air etc. are given a supernatural, religio-theological coating and one comes across the speculation of *devas* like Agni, Baruṇa, Indra etc. So far as the Cārvāka stand is concerned, it can be noticed that it is not opposed to the admittance of the natural surrounding for the sustenance of human life. In that way, the important role of water, fire etc. cannot be gainsaid. But, being firmly rooted on the empirical footing, it has no necessity for adhering to any trans-empirical/supernatural rendering of the natural phenomena with a religio-theological coating. For, such a move lacks any evidential justification. So it is under no obligation to admit any conception of *puruṣārtha* in the transcendental sense. But, it does not follow from that the Cārvāka position is baseless and it does not accommodate any plan/design concerning human-life in general. It indicates a view of life (*weltanschauung*) that is both empirical and natural. Amidst that, it is not recalcitrant to a scheme that is quite liberal, flexible and dynamic, instead of being rigid and dogmatic. It is free and open for any change, if it is so warranted as far as the natural setting is concerned. Hence, the inculcation of the concept of *puruṣārtha* as finally aiming at *apavarga*[3] cannot be logically befitting to the Cārvāka stand. Therefore, the composition of such aphorisms (*sūtras*) in the name of Bṛhaspati seems to be a matter of interpolation and thus is incredible.

3. "*Maraṇamevapavargaḥ*" BS.8 and "*Mṛtyurevapavargaḥ*" BS30.

I. Dharma as Religion

Conceding to the point that the Cārvāka stand accommodates *kāma* and *artha* in its view of life, the issue of *dharma* is most pertinent for our present purpose of enquiry. Can a Cārvāka include *dharma* within his philosophic standpoint? It is said that to follow the dharmic procedure is unproductive.[4] There is no perceptual evidence that the dharmic practices give rise to any result as meritorious or demeritorious. Since human knowledge is primarily based on perception, the hope for attaining good result by way of performing dharmic practices turns out to be blind and baseless. Dharmic directives are supposed to provide good result in future and, in certain instances, those are also thought as to provide desired consequences in heaven (*svarga*). Since the Cārvāka stand does not entertain anything supernatural or transcendental, there is no scope for any heavenly attainment of good result. So also there is no evidence of good effects of the performance of *dharma* in view of the fact that the performer of *dharma* often faces troubles and difficulties, while a non-dharmic individual at times faces no such adverse situation. In other words, there is no necessity that dharmic acts must give rise to good results free from troubles.

The opponents have severely looked down upon the Cārvāka stand in this regard. *Dharma* traditionally has several meanings. It principally stands for (a) religion, (b) law/usage/practice, (c) religious merit/virtue, (d) duty or prescribed course of conduct, (e) right, justice, morality, etc., (f) nature/essential quality or characteristic property.[5] Out of all these, contextually two meanings can be considered as pertinent. One is the religious practice in terms of following the prescribed rites and rituals which are supposed to give rise to merits and virtues. The other stands for the observance of morality on the basis of justice, equity, impartiality and propriety.

4. "*Na dharmāścaret*" BS.9.
5. Apte, V. S. *The Student's Sanskrit - English Dictionary,* Delhi: 2000, p. 268.

According to the opponents, the Cārvāka stand fails to attain *dharma* on both the fronts.

It does not have scope for the observance of any religious practice. A Cārvāka is out and out irreligious. He does not admit the importance of rites and rituals and, accordingly, there is no room for attaining any merit or virtue. On the basis of his rejection of trans-empiric transcendence, the religious sense is set aside and, in that way, all sorts of merits and virtues are completely impossible. Thus, the Cārvāka position is held to be anti-religious and anti-dharmic (immoral). It is only designed to have maximum comfort and pleasure individually and thus the socio-religious merit or virtue is fully ruled out in its framework. So it is said to be an instance of radical egoism and selfishness.

II. Morality and Spirituality

But, such ascription needs reconsideration. So far as the Cārvāka point of view is concerned, there is no indication that it goes against social sense of morality. It never prescribes only individual pleasure at the cost of social needs and expectations. It is, of course, the case that one is to move for good and healthy food. In order to have a comfortable and balanced living, one can take loan; if it is necessary.[6] However, this never suggests that one is to have individual pleasure at the cost of others. It rather implies that at the time of need, one can make a move for loan. There is no indication that he can take loan and is not to pay it back. Taking loan by itself cannot be judged as morally reprehensible. It is said that taking loan and eating ghee (as noticed in BS) is "only allegorical, hyperbolic, sarcastic, satirical and a symbol of reactionary mood of the Chārvākas".[7] But such expression of BS need not symbolize any reactionary mood. It can be meant as directing to a valid point that taking loan in itself cannot be construed as something immoral and vicious. It is rather evident

6. "*Yāvat jīvet sukhaṁ jīivet ṛṇaṁ kṛtvā ghṛtaṁ pivet*" BS.45.
7. Prasad, S.N. *Chārvāka - Lokāyata, op.cit.*, p. 93.

that from the Cārvāka point of view, there is no suggestion for non-payment of loan. It is not necessary that "only persons who are inactive, indolent can go for loan".[8] Persons who are quite active, honest and efficient can move for loan due to certain difficult situation which is beyond their control. And, when normalcy recovers, they are eager to pay back the loan. This does happen generally and there is no moral impropriety involved in it. There is no necessary binding that the man who takes loan must be a fraud and does not care to pay back the loan to the concerned, even if he is quite capable.

Despite his critical outlook towards religio-theological dogmatic and prejudiced attitude, a Cārvāka is, however, not found to be logically committed to anti-religion. He does not advocate irreligiousness like an iconoclast. Only he is a critic of dogma, blind faith, superstition etc. which are almost embedded in all forms of religious supernatural transcendentalism and are found to be blocking the free flow of moral reasoning. It is an unwarranted customary belief in certain circle that loan is a mark of immorality and so it is sinful. Virtue and vice in the religious framework are based on some form of unwarranted transcendental presupposition. Spirit is the real individual person and he is to face either reward or punishment in his own real disembodied spiritual state. Accordingly, either he is to attain salvation or damnation.

But, it is obvious, such a dharmic recommendation is not acceptable to the Cārvāka on the ground that it is not structured on any valid reason (*hetu*). It is a surmise out of fear or wonder about the so-called status of man's being after death. On the basis of this, the socio-empiric connotation of virtue and vice is unduly extended to a trans-empirical quixotic level and some sort of spiritualization of morality has been unnecessarily advanced. It is held by the religio-theological spiritualists that true and genuine sense of morality must be grounded on some form of spiritual transcendence and, in that

8. *Ibid.*, p. 97.

way, some modern thinkers have appealed for the validity of transcendental ethics and morality.

But, it is notable that virtue and vice are squarely intelligible within the human level in its socio-empiric setting. A person can judge something as right or wrong, good or bad, just or unjust, virtuous or vicious only in its social dealings with other fellow-beings. At times, the sense of moral significance can also be extended to other animals, living plants and trees. Of course, such extension is meaningful only in and through men's relation with them in their living empirical sojourn and never beyond that. Further, the sense of morality does have its own autonomy. That is why, it is said to be sui generis. It cannot be judged as subservient to any other concept. Morality cannot be treated as an instrumental value to realize some higher goal. Because, in that way, it would bring in one odd conclusion that X practices morality because thereby he would attain some higher goal (e.g., spiritual enlightenment). In such a case, X is not moral for the sake of morality, but he follows that to have certain other goal. Of course, from this it does not follow that a spiritualist cannot be otherwise quite morally conscious in the socio-individual setting. Only it reveals that his being moral is independent of his being spiritual. The similar thing holds true in case of a materialist and others. The relation between morality and spirituality (*vice versa*) is not necessary but only contingent. This is the case because morality is a socio-empiric conceptual formulation and it has its use and operation free from any trans-empiric metaphysical speculation about the ultimate reality or the ultimate status of man in a trans-empiric state of transcendence. The Cārvāka point of view seems to be clearly opting for a free, autonomous sense of morality in the socio-individual setting of empirical significance without any transcendental conjecture and thereby it is quite consistent at the practical front. Thus *dharma* in the sense of adhering to any religious prescription for following certain rites and rituals dogmatically being based on some form of blind superstitious and romantic picture-thinking of other worldly existence has no room in the Cārvāka framework. And, for such non-acceptance of Vedic rites and rituals, the Cārvāka stand need not be branded as immoral and unjust.

It is held that the Vedic tradition is firmly rooted on human welfare in general (*sarve sukhinaḥ bhavantu* etc.). It is not egoistic in the sense of only aiming at individual happiness and pleasure. It does not oppose non-violence (*ahiṁsā*) not only for men but for all living beings (*jīvedayā*). There is some scriptural sources in which such altruistic moves are hailed. But, it is also to be marked that there are many other references which are grossly incompatible with such moves as referred to above. The Vedic/Vedāntic ideal for attaining *mukti* or *mokṣa* is for the concerned individual, who is even directed to aspire for such goal, completely ignoring his socio-human responsibilities, family obligations and turns out to be an escapist so far as the normal worldly life (*saṁsāra*) is concerned. He does not care to attend his socio-moral duties and responsibilities. He even does not hesitate to leave his family and friends in distress for his own stubborn desire for attaining liberated enlightenment (*mumukṣu*).[9] Such a move cannot justifiably be treated as free from egoistic limitations. Again, the Vedic recommendation for killing of animals and even men before the sacrificial altar with the blind supposition that such sacrifices would yield good results to people is squarely immoral and unjust. In this regard, the Vedic protagonist's remark that the Vedic violence is not real violence (*vaidiki hiṁsā, hiṁsā na bhavati*) does not carry conviction. A Cārvāka seems to be justified in challenging such ghastly religious practices. It is a pity that even now the sacrifice of animals before the altar or deity still continues (though not so widely). On many other cases, there is the

9. Buddha's leaving his wife (Yaśodhārā), son and family secretly in the dead of the night to move outside for the search of enlightenment, Rāma's sending his pregnant wife: Sītā to the dense forest secretly (without letting her know) only on the pretext of unproved allegation made by one commoner are the gruesome challenging moral issues in this context.

substitute of animal sacrifice by sacrifice of fruits (like breaking coconut). Such change, though less offensive, carries the stigma of blind faith in some form or the other. The Cārvāka stand is found to be morally justified in raising its voice against such acts of violence and amply reveals its social concern. It is not at all infatuated with gross sense of egoistic feeling but is quite in tune with the general sense of compassion and proper dealings with living beings.[10] Hence, the use of *dharma* in the sense of dogmatically practicing gruesome religious practices can never be the mark of moral consciousness. In that sense, Cārvāka is justifiably against *dharma.*[11]

III. The Naturalistic Conception of Morality

But the other meaning of *dharma* which has definite traditional usage and legitimate sanction does vindicate the moral sense of justice, equity and propriety etc. in the socio-individual empirical plane. It is not bound by religio-theological restriction but is distinctly moral. It is founded on socio-individually acceptable norms which are formulated in the background of universality and, at the same time, are liberal, flexible and dynamic, keeping in tune with the situation and remain firm in its operation. There is no reference that the Cārvāka is only for his own happiness and comfort at the cost of pains and sufferings of others. It faces those calmly and tries to overcome those by available means and applying skill and intelligence. The empirical devices are sought and no such transcendental speculative surmises are entertained which are not only unverifiable by empirical procedure but also are not logically tenable. Those are the outcome of romantic imagination mostly capitalizing upon the naive sense of fear, wonder and cheap sentiment.

The generally accepted Vedic view-point is held to advocate the naturalistic conception of morality. The nature is viewed as

10. "*Paṣuścennihataḥ svarge jyotiṣṭome gamiṣyati sva pitā yajamānena tatra kasmānna hanyate.*" B.S. 41.
11. BS.9.

morally inbuilt. The concept of *ṛta* is supposed to be encompassing the whole natural phenomena. The moral rule governs the whole universe. The same principle of *ṛta* is later on applied to human life and the concept of *karma* is evolved to explain the individual's life and his situational placement. From the Cārvāka point of view, the Vedic presupposition is found to be logically unfounded. For, nature with its mechanism on one hand and morality along with its implication of duty and obligations on the other hand are clearly different and distinct. Normally nature seems to operate uniformly; but there are exceptions. The mechanics of natural operation is not necessarily fixed and static. But, in case of the use and application of morality, there is no such implication. Commitment to morality is self-dependent. It is not conditioned or determined by any external factor. That is why; it is logically related to duty and obligation of the agent. Either the sense of avoiding the duties or not complying with one's own obligations is never construed as morally sacrosanct. The moral sense of accomplishing duty can be the effect of one's own decision or judgment; because duty is not the effect of any external source. If one is morally convinced of something to be his duty and that is to be performed, then that is the end of it. It is not because of his physical strength or muscle-power. It is a mental resolve which he undertakes being fully guided by a moral will and conviction, of course not thereby hampering or adversely affecting others.[12] The Cārvāka stand never gives any scope for evading moral responsibility. It does not speak against family or even social obligations. So to treat the Cārvāka position as out and out immoral and that as grossly set for attaining egoistic pleasure and fulfilment of passions and carnal desires at the cost of humanity is not rationally tenable. It is rightly held that the Cārvāka stand is neither for aggressive sex nor for sex-repression.[13] Balanced attitude towards

12. *Vide*, in this connection, the penetrative analysis of the concepts of varṇadharma and varṇāśrama dharma by Rajendra Prasad in his *Varṇadharma, Niṣkāma Karma and Practical Morality*, D.K. Printworld (P) Ltd., New Delhi, 1999.
13. Prasad, S.N., *op.cit.*, p. 93.

sex and other socio-individual transactions is never opposed. Thereby the sense of one's duty and obligation in the moral framework is well retained.

IV. Varṇadharma

The classification of men into four fundamental groups is referred to in the Vedic source and later on it is widely endorsed in other sources including *Bh. Gītā.* In the religious circle, such classification is traditionally accepted and a moral coating is grafted on such four-fold division (*caturvarga*). We, however, do not come across of any direct critical remark on the four-fold division in the BS. But, nonetheless, there is found to be no indication about its approval. Rather the rational enterprise introduced and carried out in the Cārvāka stand amply indicates that such classification of men is, acceptable within its framework, neither logically nor morally. The implication of the Cārvāka point of view can be drawn as follows.

The classification is not logical on the ground that each member is not exclusive of the other. On the contrary, those are meaningfully overlapping. A Brahmin is found as a warrior and a Vaiśya as an enlightened person (e.g., Droṇācārya and Raikva). The attempt of defending the classification as the creation of Lord Kṛṣṇa Himself is unacceptable to the Cārvāka stand not simply because it cannot accommodate any trans-empirical/transcendental justification of the division —which are purely *svabhāvaja*; but because of the fact that the nature of man is rather based on the circumstantial factors in the empirical setting and is not due to any transcendental source. That is why the nature found in him in one setting is changed in another setting. Further, the fourth group i.e., Śudra does not have any specific duty to perform but is only to serve (*paricaryātmakaṁ*) the other three cited groups is not only logically incongruent but it is also morally questionable and blameworthy.

The Cārvāka stand never advocates for happiness with any sense of caste discrimination. It does not plead for any personal gain by offering sacrifices to a transcendental deity, like aspiring for a son in order to cross over hell (*puṁ nāma narakāt trāyate iti putraḥ*). In the social dealings, Cārvāka does not vindicate any escapist or negative attitude; but, on the contrary, has a positive, life-affirming stance so that the normal man retains a calm, balanced tempered state without tampering the general sense of peace and harmony so far as socio-individual relationship is concerned. There is no indication that he opts for a slothful living. Instead of manual and mental labour, it does not preach any visionary romanticism about the other-world and it never pleads for begging as a dignified form of living which is so encouraged and approved among the priestly group (*bhavat bhikṣāṁ dehī*). A mendicant or a sanyāsin's living is not a matter of dignity. The moral expectation is rather in favour of doing some physical and mental labour and to earn one's livelihood by means of that. Even it is well marked that many handicapped and disabled persons make all possible effort to be self-dependent and they never feel happy to be a burden on others. If such a situation occurs which is beyond their control, they accept other's help with much agony and reluctance. It is quite evident that a Cārvāka is prone to morality in the usual normal sense.

V. Happiness and Morality

On the basis of the aforesaid discussion, it can be seen that the Cārvāka stand is not averse to *Dharma* in the sense of morality. The Cārvāka textual source has not detailed out the ethical basis of its sense of morality. But that does not philosophically matter much. For, one can draw out the logical implication of its stray remark on morality and thereby its moral philosophy can be formed and brought to focus. As it is seen, it is fully inappropriate to identify Cārvāka as hedonist either in the gross or in the refined sense. His reference to happiness (*sukha*) is not aimed at gross sensual pleasure in the sexual sense. Of course, there is mention about *kāma* in BS and it has been also cited in different sources. *Kāma*, in one of its primary senses, means love or desire of sensual enjoyments. At times it points to desire of carnal gratification and lust. However, in a general sense, it is also used as connoting wish, desire and affection.[14] So far as the Cārvāka stand is taken into account, *kāma* is, of course, duly recognized as important in human life and that is nothing abnormal or unnatural. As a matter of fact, the normal man has the inclination for affection, desire, love and wish inclusive of gratification. So to include that as one of the facets of life is not something surprising.

However, it is notable that for Cārvāka, *Kāma* is not necessarily confined to carnal desire and it includes within its fold all sorts of desire. To seek for happiness or to desire for pleasure, in this sense, is something quite normal. Even the spiritualists like Advaita Vedāntins regard *mokṣa* as a desire (*mumukṣu*). Because pleasure gives happiness and pain gives unhappiness which includes sorrows and sufferings, the classical Indian philosophers (*darśanajñas*) emphasize on the cessation of sorrows (*duḥkha*) and thereby they have the indirect proneness for happiness. But, some of them, on account of their spiritualistic bias, prefer another elevated expression: bliss (*parama sukha/ānanda*). Thereby an attempt has been made to distinguish between ordinary happiness (*laukika sukha*) and pure unalloyed happiness or bliss.

But, it can be well marked that such a conception of bliss is something designed to be applicable to a soul / spirit/ self (*ātmā*) in the trans-empirical sense. So, obviously there is no scope for permanent/eternal bliss in the Cārvāka framework which never transgresses the ordinary commonsensical socio-human empiric framework, not simply because such conception does not have empirical validity but also it is not convincing on account of lack of reason. In other words, the trans-empiric speculation about self being in the state of transcendental bliss is logically unwarranted. The Cārvāka position treats happiness as desirable in and through the empiric living and it never aspires for any absolute happiness bereft

14. Apte, V.S., *op.cit.,* p. 143.

of sorrows and sufferings. It seems that the Cārvāka point of view is well settled. It does not negate sorrows and sufferings in human life. Only it perhaps aptly reminds that it is natural and practical to minimize pain as far as possible and to desire for pleasure/happiness and peace in the socio-individual setting. In that sense, there is the acceptance of *kāma* as just acknowledging the role of love, affection desire and wish, not thereby simply insisting on the adoption of carnal gratification leaving aside other legitimate needs and requirements in the socio-individual plane. Thus the Cārvāka stand is in tune with the background of human welfare.

Neither pain by itself nor pleasure by itself is morally a vice or a virtue respectively. Only when any voluntary action or thought is advanced with bad or good intention/motive it is graded as immoral or moral on the basis of certain norm in the midst of socio-individual relationship. Both pain and pleasure happen to a person either due to him or due to circumstance/situation in which he happens to be. The ascription of moral sense is plausible over the decision/judgment and the consequent action that the person undertakes either individually or in a group. And for all that he is found to be morally accountable. The Cārvāka position, it can be held, is not outside the general sense of morality. Pleasure is not, for a Cārvāka, the norm of goodness. Therefore, the doctrine of ethical hedonism seems to be clearly inapplicable to his framework. Not only *kāma* but also *artha* is recognized by the Cārvākas for the smooth run of human life. This has, of course, a practical bearing and need not be disparaged. A man, in the normal setting, needs the implementation of both reasonably and there is no impropriety in this. Only the excessive desire for the fulfilment of one's wish etc. and to go after wealth and to amass it beyond one's legitimate needs and requirements bring in anxiety, tension and torment. Further, it also creates imbalance in the social dealings, causing thereby hatred, strife and troubles. Consequently, there results in some sort of practical hazard and that are morally not innocuous too.

VI. The Socio-Human Account of Morality

On the basis of the analytical scrutiny of the Cārvāka stand, it can be maintained that it has duly acknowledged the important role of both *kāma* and *artha* in human life. Nevertheless, one thing should be noted that in its framework, both of them cannot be construed as *puruṣārthas* in the sense that those are not ideal aims of life. Their utilitarian value in the non-moral pragmatic sense is never thereby denigrated. But all that need not be confounded with the sense of morality. To be moral, within the Cārvāka framework, does neither signify exclusive utilitarian value in the popular sense of pragmatic advantage nor does it imply aiming at the attainment of a spiritual ideal. It seems to be far away from both the radical versions of cheap populism and also fanciful spiritual idealism. *Dharma* as morality is neither assimilated with the attainment of sole pleasure or maximum pleasure at the cost of others legitimate due nor is even equated with the performances of religio-theologically prescribed rites and rituals in order to attain quixotic absolute freedom/liberation (*mukti*). From the Cārvāka perspective, *dharma* is meaningful only in the context of men in the worldly set up. It is related to the world in which human beings live. It is applicable to man in his socio-empiric existence and never beyond that in a supra-mundane transcendent disembodied spiritual state of existence.

Man is viewed as a social being in the Cārvāka framework. The issue of *dharma* is significant in respect of man-in-society. Of course, the term: society has some special implication here. Society does not mean something static and immobile. Its status is amenable to change as per the existing situation and also taking into account the attitude, taste and temperament of its members, coming in contact with different people belonging to other ethnic group/social sectors. There is ample scope for cross social interrelationship. And, that in turn, gives rise to cultural, intellectual exchange, resulting in revision of attitudes etc. In that way, socio-individual expectations, needs and requirements move on being modified from time to time.

Thereby, society becomes liberal; open textured and is prone to reform, of course, not dispensing with moral reasoning. The logical implication of the Cārvāka stand vindicates that any moral norm or principle be so ordained that it must be instantiable. That means, if the moral norm can never be practiced or operated in thought as well as action, then such a norm becomes nothing but a fanciful ideal. It may have romantic charm but can never be convincing from the point of view of balanced moral reasoning. In order to be instantiated, the norm must be applicable in and through the socio-individual transaction. It is true that 'ought' cannot be derived from 'is', though 'ought' implies 'can' in a specific sense. Even if value is not derived from fact, yet it is applicable to factual dealings. After all, values are comprehended and are worked out by man in his socio-empiric set up and not otherwise. In this context, perhaps, Wittgenstein's remark that ethics does not treat the world; it must be a condition of the world like logic is insightful. The Cārvāka position never treats moral value to be either trans-human or trans-empirical. It is meaningful in and through man's socio-empiric existence. It is applicable significantly to man's action and thought in his multifarious socio-individual dealings.

VII. Freedom and Morality

Some thinkers have emphasized on freedom in the concept of morality. It is, as already indicated, morality that is free and is not obsequious to any other external source. It cannot be treated as instrument for the accomplishment of any higher end. That is why, the rendering of *kāma, artha* and *dharma* as instrumental values for *mokṣa* - the ultimate end or goal is not logically sound. On this point, an attempt has been drawn in certain quarters to interpret the concept of morality in the metaphysical sense of absolutism. That means, moral freedom implies absoluteness or perfection in the fullest sense. So far as the Cārvāka philosophical position is concerned, such a radical, uncompromising sense of freedom is not logically compelling. Conceding that freedom is necessary for the operation of moral norm or ethical principle, it, of course, concedes the sense of universality. Speaking truth is universally held as a moral virtue. So there is no oddity in pronouncing "Speaking truth is good" as an instance of moral judgment. But, all the same, there are cases where one is under obligation not to speak truth but to ignore it for some greater cause which again is moral. A higher moral consideration leaves room for some exceptional cases where there is the need for a review, taking the circumstantial factors into account. However, such exceptional case does not rub out the universal feature of moral reasoning. It only points out that exceptional moral decision carries also the sense of universality. Variance in moral decision does not curtail its tone of freedom; only radical sense of absolute and ultimate freedom is, in this regard, critically dealt with.

The Cārvāka stand never challenges the social cohesion or integrity in the general form. If there is no cohesion and harmony in the social group or community, then the members do not have peace. There is the continuance of mutual distrust and consequently morality both at individual and social level becomes heavily affected. So to retain stability in social order and discipline, the role of individuals therein is of great importance. They need to conduct themselves in such a manner so that the sense of peaceful co-existence and fellow-feeling takes a concrete shape. Thus, moral life is of practical necessity and not an ideal chimera in the sense of transcendence. The Cārvāka point of view, it seems, is quite concerned about this socio-human moral responsibility and its practical importance. In this way, the prospect of applied ethics is very much latent in its philosophical outlook. It is prone to a non-feudal and secular view of life based on liberal moral foundation of human significance. The Cārvāka sense of morality is not set for following any theoretical abstract sense of visionary idealism, but, on the contrary, it is keen on following that moral norms which have practical bearing in man's life in the empiric setting. The suggestion that the earlier view of three-fold classification of *kāma, artha* and *dharma* is acceptable to the Cārvāka position requires a review. For, *dharma* is never set on par with both *artha* and *kāma*. While both of them are acceptable from pragmatic angle, those are not desired with an aim to be moral. To move for acquiring wealth is useful for the smooth run of living. So also inclination for love, wish etc. is not undesirable but is quite natural. But *dharma* is necessary in human life, not simply it is pragmatically efficacious. It involves the inculcation of finer sense of rational conscience that aims at discharging one's duties and responsibilities. It has an implication of fulfilling one's obligations and he is not hesitant to be accountable. *Dharma* includes all such modes of operation so far as man-in-society is concerned. In case of wish, desire etc. there is no moral involvement, though those are quite relevant in his social dealings. Those grow in man out of his intense emotion and sentiment towards certain object/person. So also acquisition of wealth to certain degree is definitely required for smooth living. But the requirement in both the cases is not necessarily moral. Both *kāma* and *artha* are desired for non-moral purposes too, while *dharma* has independent grounding both in thought and action without any ulterior motive or intention. It is out of one's own conviction or will, without expecting anything in return. It is not followed by an individual on the basis that praise and admiration would be bestowed on him in return; though they may occur in some cases. Moral will is conducted and moral progress is made independent of such consequences.

The moral outlook in the Cārvāka framework is not thus construed as a mark of escapism, life-negating and is bound by trans-social ties and transactions. It is avowedly optimistic, practical and quite reasonable.

CĀRVĀKA AND SELF

In the present work, both the words: Cārvāka and Lokāyata are used interchangeably, conceding that the use of Lokāyata is usually treated as earlier to that of Cārvāka.[1] Bṛhaspati is generally accepted as the founder of the Cārvāka/Lokāyata view-point, though it is also noticed that there are references about number of Bṛhaspati in the tradition.[2] Out of which mainly one comes across two Bṛhaspatis in *Ṛg Veda* - one pointing to Aṅgirasa and another to Laukya.[3] It is found that Aṅgirasa is a celebrated sage and to whom many hymns are ascribed. Bṛhaspati is the preceptor of devas (*devaguru*).[4] Laukya means mundane/human/common/profane. Accordingly, Bṛhaspati is regarded as the primary advocate of ***nāstika*** or Cārvāka/Lokāyata view-point.[5]

A Vedic reference indicates that out of non-existence (*asat*), existence (*sat*) comes into being.[6] At a much later date, it is interpreted that the Lokāyata/Cārvāka stand takes *asat* as matter (*jaḍa*) and *sat* as consciousness (*caitanya*). And it holds that consciousness is produced out of matter.[7] Accordingly, it is widely thought that the Cārvāka stand is only materialistic and it does not accept spirit/soul/self in any manner. Such a rendering of the

1. *cf. Lokāyata-sūtra,* referred to by Guṇaratna in his *Saḍ darśanasamuccaya and Cārvāka-sūtra* referred to by Abhayadevasuri in his gloss *(ṭīkā)* on *Tarkaprakaraṇa.*
2. *Vide*, for details, S. Pathak: *Cārvāk Darśankī Śāstrīya Samīkṣā, op. cit.,* pp.64-72.
3. Ṛg. Veda, *10,72,2.*
4. V.S. Apte: *op.cit.,* p. 394 and p. 485.
5. *'Brāhaspatyastu nāstikaḥ'* - Hemacandra : *Abhidhāna Cintāmoṇiḥ.*
6. 'asat idaṁ agra āsit'.
7. *"Sat Brahmavarga: asat jadavarga"*
   Nāgoji Bhaṭṭ, commentator on *Durgāsaptaśatī,* 1.62.

Cārvāka philosophy is commonly taken for granted. Previously, critical discussion regarding the ascription of materialism to the Cārvāka view-point has been dealt with. Here, an attempt is being made to critically evaluate the Cārvāka position as pointing to the denial of self.

I. *Asat* as *Jaḍa*

First of all, treating *asat* as *jaḍa* and *sat* as *caitanya* does not seem to be that simple and unambiguous. Lexically *asat* means non-existent/unreal. It also contextually stands for something as bad, wrong, improper, false, unchaste, not manifest etc.[8] But to reduce the sense of *asat* to *jaḍa* (i.e., cold, dull, motionless, stupid, irrational, devoid of appreciation, taste and the like) is not unquestionable. Because characterizing something to be cold, dull, stupid, irrational, idiot etc. are cogently applicable to persons, having normal sense of awareness and response. If the person does not respond to certain stimuli normally, he is generally judged as dull and stupid etc. It does not make sense to attribute matter or material products as dull, stupid, irrational etc.

Again, while the word : *asat* is meant as non-existent/unreal, it is clearly a descriptive account and, in that way, it is different from its being used as bad, wrong, improper etc. because the characterization of bad, improper etc. are precisely evaluative and not descriptive. For instance, if an Advaitin holds the world (*saṅsāra*) as illusory (*mithyā/māyā*) then this does not give a description of what the world actually is but how the world is to be viewed from a specific dārśanic (philosophical) view-point. Even treating *asat* as not manifest (and taking *sat* as manifest by contrast) carries the suggestion of a metaphysical stand that the effect is *asat* in the cause only in the sense of being not manifest and not in the sense of its being non-existent or unreal. In this manner, the metaphysical stand (*satkāryavāda*) is found to be opposed to the other metaphysical stand

8. V.S. Apte, *op.cit.*, p. 69.

that the effect is non-existent in the cause and it is originated as *sat* only as effect. *Asatkāryavāda* does not subscribe to the metaphysical speculation of pre-existence of effect prior to its origination. So to some, *asat* stands for not manifest and *sat* stands for manifest. Both these attributions are metaphysically loaded evaluation, far from the descriptive content. Thus both the descriptive and evaluative uses of the words: *sat/asat* need to be deciphered in this respect.

The different uses that are current in respect of the word: *jaḍa* are found to be quite effective in conveying contextual evaluation. For instance, the room is cold to a person, directly coming from the open-field during mid-day of summer season; while the same room is found to be not cold but warm to another person, coming directly from one ice-chamber. In other words, all such attributions have contextual evaluative significance. So also the characterization of appreciation, taste etc. are obviously evaluative with reference to the person concerned taking into account several factors like situation, person's response to the stimuli as per his ability/efficiency. But, in any case, all these meanings that are associated with the word: *jaḍa* carry referential significance to normal living person and never to something as pure motionless matter as such. Such an extension of the meaning of the word: *jaḍa* seems to lose its significance altogether. Hence, the attempt to read the Vedic concept of *asat* as *jaḍa* and that again as matter, contrasting it from *sat* (suggesting it to be *caitanya* or consciousness) seems to be somewhat obscure and misleading. It does (as indicated before) need reconsideration.

II. Denial of Self

There is wide spread advocacy that the Cārvākas deny soul/self altogether. They do not accept the existence of *ātmā*. The opponents hold that, according to the Cārvākas, there is no world (*loka*) like heaven (*svarga*) and hell (*narka*), besides this world (*iha loka*).[9] Such

9. *"Ihalokātparo nānyaḥ, svarga nāsti narako na ca"* - Śaṅkarācārya in his *Sarva Siddhānta Saṅgraha.*

an exposition is based on the heavily publicized assumption that the Cārvāka accepts sense-perception as the only source of knowing. The sensible world is accepted on account of its being perceived. True, one does not come across the detailed account of the Cārvāka stand on the foundation of knowledge-claim. It is only made explicit that it gives emphasis on empirical knowledge and does not accept any claim for trans-empirical supra-sensible transcendental knowledge. In other words, any knowable object is asserted to be within the empirical fold.

Now, what does this empirical foundation of knowledge imply? Does it necessarily suggest that what alone is sense-perceived at present that is the object of knowledge and nothing else? Previously, we have offered detailed discussion on the Cārvāka stand on knowledge. It is clear that according to the logical frame of the Cārvāka stand, the knowable object is not simply confined to what is known but also to what is in principle knowable through empirical means. The world as a whole or in its totality is never sense-perceived. The future occurrence of fire in the forest during heavy summer is not now sense-perceived. But that does not preclude those to be empirical and the knowledge-claim of such occurrence is never ruled out in the Cārvāka scheme. The empirical generalization on the basis of past experiences is well accommodated. Even if the whole world is not seen, yet it becomes empirically relevant in view of the combination of both sense-perceived data/contents and the empiric constructs. It is by the copulation of both content and construct, the ordinary empirical objects of knowledge are formed and thereby the sense-perceptual foundation of empirical knowledge never gets ruptured. That is why the Cārvāka stand is not opposed to inference which is primarily sense-bound. But, any trans-empirical extension of inference to something supra-sensible and transcendental is not acceptable within the Cārvāka framework.

Moreover the term: reality can be made intelligible within the empirical domain. One can perfectly distinguish between something as real and something else as appearance in the perceptual field. But from this, to make a sweep that either everything is nothing but only real or that is nothing but mere appearance is logically neither admissible nor warranted. The Cārvāka stand, it seems, is clearly on solid logical ground in determining the legitimate bounds of sense and knowledge. It never opts for any metaphysical reductionist thesis that either everything is real or everything is unreal. In fact, it does not have any scope for trans-empiric ontological presupposition.

It is in this background; its denial of self (*ātmā*) can be properly estimated. It does deny any trans-empirical knowledge-claim of any supra-sensible entity/being. It neither has any *a priori* affirmation nor denial of the existence of such objects. Only it asserts that the knowledge-claim of such entities/beings is not based on reason (*hetu*). Whatever is not feasible within the scope of knowledge in the usual sense of the term, any attempt to make any assertion regarding that (either positive or negative) is nothing but turns out to be wild surmise. Thus the denial self, in this regard, only points to a particular conception or theory of self, i.e. a pure trans-empirical, transcendental being, devoid of body, mind and senses and yet is ever pure conscious. The self, according to the set view, is held to be a self-conscious being (*jīvātmā*) which moves from one body to another body, from one birth to another birth and it continues to have its sameness or identity without any break. Again, as per some metaphysical speculation, such disembodied self-conscious being is held to be non-different from absolute pure Being/Spirit (*ātmā*).

It is evident that the Cārvāka stand does not find any logical justification for admitting such a notion of self. It argues that such a self devoid of body etc. is simply inconceivable. There cannot be any cognition/recognition, identification/reidentification, awareness/self-awareness of a disembodied person. Such mental occurrences are meaningfully comprehended in and through empirical living situation. All this, however, does not necessitate the conclusion that the Cārvāka stand is opposed to the admittance of self in its common ordinary use.

III. The Cārvāka Account of Self

At the common sense level, there is a valid distinction between myself and others. A person, while referring to his needs and requirements as different from other person's belongings and necessities, becomes self-aware or self-conscious. It may also be the case that one is at times both self-conscious and also conscious of others. While driving a vehicle, one may think about himself and also looks at the road for safe-driving. However, there is no conceptual oddity in distinguishing self-awareness and other-awareness, despite the point that those occur together on many occasions normally.

The Cārvāka stand does not question the legitimacy of such conceptual distinction. The commonsense notion is well adopted in social, physical and biological sciences. There is no incongruity in acknowledging the distinction between myself and others. In this sense, the Cārvāka position never stands counter to common sense and also to science. But, when a metaphysically loaded peculiar notion of self as pure spirit/disembodied soul as the real person is introduced by the opponents, the Cārvāka position stands against it. In this connection, one finds references of bodied-self (*dehātmā*), sense-bound self (*indriyātmā*), mind-involved conscious self (*manaścaitanyātmā*) and life-bound self (*prāṇātmā*) in the traditional sources.

Mādhavācārya, while exposing the Cārvāka view, has maintained that the soul is not different from body. The expressions like 'I am fat' etc. do not suggest that 'I' myself is different from body; it only means 'I' as the body is fat. It is like 'Rāhu's head' where Rāhu is not fully different from head; but the head itself in a specific sense is Rāhu. In other words, the expression: Rāhu's head is only a matter of figurative succession.[10]

---

10. *Vide* his Sarva Darśana Saṅgraha, 1.63-64.

It seems, the explanation that is offered by the celebrated author of the medieval period does not bring out the logical import of the Cārvāka view accurately. It is true that a Cārvāka does not subscribe to the remark that self is to be construed as existing entity totally different from body; but it also does not mean thereby that self is nothing else but the body alone. The very fact of one being self-conscious as well as other-conscious clearly reveals that the individual or the normal person (as long as he lives) makes a valid distinction between himself and his body with its different parts including the different sense/motor organs and even mind. Supposing, for some reason or the other, one organ is found to be defunct, then the person does not cease to have his personal identity (despite the organ being fully damaged). Hence, at the common sense plane, (which is also not unreasonable), there is no oddity in distinguishing between himself and his body. But all this is cogent and intelligible as long as the person lives as a normal conscious living individual. The meaning of self is well retained only in and through the empiricality and never transcending that. Even the term: spirit is treated as quite plausible within the empiric framework, and its so called transcendental ontological existence as fully free and independent being/entity thus appears to be woolly and incomprehensible.

Perhaps, it is in this background, the characterization of the Cārvāka philosophical point of view as treating self (*ātmā*) in terms of body, sense, mind, consciousness and life can be found as plausible. It does not thereby maintain that the self is identical with either the body or the organ (sense/motor), or the mind (*manas*) or the vital air (*prāṇa*) as such. It rather points to another significant issue that the very concept of self is meaningfully applied in and through all these facets and never completely transcending those in some quixotic from of transcendental existence. The empirical totality is clearly adhered to without implying thereby the absolute indispensability of each one of them singly. When the person is dead, obviously there is no sense in saying that the person continues to have either self-identity or other-identity. That is the significance of the saying: death is the end of existence. In that sense, he being a normal self-conscious person ceases to exist. But that does not entail that other living individuals/friends and relatives fail to identify him and pay tribute to the dead person. So, even if the life ceases to exist, the dead body is identified as the body of such a person (self) who was there previously and is no more at present. That means, the use and application of the concept of self is quite sound within the empiric bounds and never beyond that.

When one pays tribute to a dead person, he obviously does not mean the dead body. The customary expression: let his bereaved soul remain in peace is a figurative one, having least literal significance. A picture of the dead person (i.e. the presentation of his body as a mark of identity) is only treated as a symbol through which the dead one's past (i.e. as an empirically living person, his thoughts and actions including his effective achievements and contributions) is remembered with gratitude. In all such instances, person is taken into account which is, of course, not disembodied (and also not just identical with body). A physical body, though, is a necessary accompanying feature, is not same as person. And a person, though not identical with the body, senses etc., cannot be conceived as fully an independent spiritual being having its continuity in a purely disembodied form of existence.

Perhaps, that is the sense of constraint on account of which some classical Indian philosophers have found the necessity of introducing subtle body (*sūkhma śarīra*) which is supposed to carry the individual soul (*jīvātmā*) from its earthly existence (*iha loka sattā*) to a trans-empiric other-worldly existence (*para loka sattā*). Even, in tradition, *devas/devīs* (usually referred to as gods and goddesses) are presumed to be bodied not disembodied. The humanized conception of theistic idols seems to be a special feature of the Hindu religious framework.

IV. Epiphenomenalism and Cārvāka

An ascription is made on the Cārvāka/Lokāyata stand that consciousness, according to it, is emerged out of the primary elements (*bhūta*). This account strikingly resembles the theory of epiphenomenalism that mind/consciousness is the by-product of matter. But from this the oft drawn conclusion (as advanced in certain circle, especially by the opponents) that the Cārvāka stand has no scope for the legitimate use of the concept of self in the common discourse does not logically follow. As expressed earlier, the Cārvāka position is against the particular theory of self (as supported by the spiritual transcendentalists) but not the concept of self as current in the ordinary discourse.

In the usual meaningful conversation, the concept of self is found to be genuine and its legitimacy cannot be gainsaid. Only what is its scope and limit of application that needs elucidation and exploration. The Cārvāka stand can be reviewed and its logical implication can be drawn accordingly. The concept: self is very much conceded in the Cārvāka framework in view of the term: *ātmā* being referred to again and again. Only the concept has been analyzed in terms of its actual use in the common discourse, without attempting to make a dive into the supra-empirical transcendence. Self is reduced neither to body nor to matter. It is a proper concept, having its own autonomy; but its application is also not unlimited in order to carry the sense of eternal (*kūṭasthanitya*) and unchangeable pure existence (*apariṇāmī śuddha sattā*). Self stands for person and, in this sense, its individuality and privacy is well acknowledged. But, at the same time, it does not imply that the self as an individual is purely exclusive and it exists fully being self-sufficient without others. Self-consciousness is possible only amidst other things and beings. That means, self-awareness need not be reduced to radical sense of ego-centricity, fully disregarding other selves within the socio-human framework. In the moral plane, the sense of self-sacrifice is significant to the extent that the self is reasonably concerned about others' welfare. But, that again, does not entail that self-sacrifice is no way proper if it does not end in self-murder. That is why, the Cārvāka stand is well concerned with common human happiness in the reasonable background with due regard to the maintenance of equilibrium so far as socio-individual bond is considered.

The Vedāntins in general subscribe to the view of self (*ātmān=a-at-man*) as eternal (*śāśvata*) and indestructible (*abināśī*). It is the essence or central core (*bījakoṣa*) of anything whatsoever. It is the innermost real or ultimate reality (*parama sattā*) i.e. Brahman. The individual souls (*jīvātmās*) are construed either as non-different from Brahman (*paramātman*) (i.e., Advaita) or as part (*aṁśa*) of Brahman (i.e. Viśiṣṭādvaita). Opposed to this, there is the reference of another view regarding self (*anātma/nairātmya vāda*). According to that, there is nothing like eternal entity/being as the essence. Real is that which changes incessantly (*yat kṣaṇikaṁ tat sat*). It is not the sense of essentiality (*śāśvata bhāva*) but the sense of inessentiality (*nisvabhāva*) that is regarded as the approved one. Such a view is found in Buddhism (at least in its early phase - cf. the dialogue between Milinda king and Nāgaśena) where no inner substantive entity is admitted over and above the different modes (No wheel as such is admitted as being there apart from axle, spoke etc.). This is contrasted from the Upaniṣadic account of the charioteer as distinct independent being apart from the chariot.[11] From such a view-point, the theory of momentariness (*kṣaṇabhaṅgavāda*) is advanced.

Now, what is the implication of this view? Does it suggest that ultimately reality is nothing but momentary? In other words, is Buddhist philosophy committed to one *a priori* theory in the background of inessentiality? In view of Buddha's abstinence from making any remark (either positive or negative) about the metaphysical queries, it rather clearly reveals his disavowal for any

---

11. *"Ātmānaṁ rathināṁ viddhiḥ śarīraṁ-rathaṁeva tu"* - Kaṭha Upaniṣad, I.III.3.

a priori metaphysical theorization. The doctrine of momentariness, therefore, seems to imply that nothing appears to be everlasting in the sense of pointing to any unchanging eternal substance/entity or being. From this remark, nothing is entailed that ultimate reality is only momentary. It is never construed as a metaphysical substitute for eternalism. While the latter is a metaphysically derived conclusion, the former is the outcome of some sort of analysis in the phenomenal plane.

It is at the backdrop of momentariness, the implication of non-substantiality and inessentiality can be probed. It seems that both the conceptual formulations point to the non-acceptance of the reality of any substantive being/self. There is no justification for admitting any substantive entity as eternally existing in view of experiencing the transitory and fleeting character of the phenomenal order. If this is conceded, then one can conclude that the view of *anātma/ nairātmya* as no-self-points only to the lack of justification for the metaphysical claim of the reality of substantial being and thereby it never aims at providing another metaphysical theory of ultimate reality. No-self (*anātma*) is not another rival metaphysical doctrine. It only points to the logical unsoundness of such metaphysical theory of reality.

Now, let the Cārvāka critical stand on the theory of self be reflected upon. It is true that a Cārvāka never accepts the trans-empirical account of self as ultimately real being. It rules out the existential claim of any transcendental speculative entity or entities on logical ground. But, as already hinted before, it does not thereby reject the concept of self as used in the commonsensical parlance. The ordinary commonsensical notion of self as pointing to person with his bodily features as well as mental traits and dispositions is well taken care of. Such an account of the concept of person does not provoke individualism/egoism. On the contrary, it is well in tune with the expectation of social set up.

One thing, however, is to be noted here. The Cārvāka account of self does neither reduce it to mere body nor to the material elements (*bhūta*) as is presumed in certain quarters. It does admit the uniqueness of normal self in the empirical plane that is capable of thinking, feeling and willing. It has the capacity for making choice, deliberation, decision, judgment etc. All this is taken up by self as a person and not by mere body; but from this also, the trans-empirical, absolutely independent disembodied existence of self as person is not implied. The Cārvāka stand, therefore, limits the meaningful use of the concept of self within the empiric fold. And, in this respect, its stand is closer to the Buddhist point of view than to the Vedic standpoint. However, there is a remarkable difference between the Buddhist and the Cārvāka view-points, insofar as the former is (as exposed in some Buddhist circle) to favour (rather incoherently) some sort of fluid self and its being regulated by the law of *karma* that is extended to several births. But the latter does not have any valid ground for the admittance of self along with the idea of its being transmigrated and reborn.

CĀRVĀKA AND SOCIO-INDIVIDUAL RELATIONSHIP

As already hinted before, the Cārvāka stand has been castigated both by traditional and modern writers as grossly immoral and having no concern for a noble as well as stable social life. It is mostly presented as crass, ego-centred and opportunistic hedonism. Accordingly, it is viewed as futile to explore any socio-individual relationship within the Cārvāka framework. Such a point of view seems to have been unopposed mainly in view of scanty availability of Cārvāka source-material. And, moreover, the Cārvāka stand, being radically different from the strongly publicized, spiritual outlook, is placed far away from the mainstream and is earmarked as providing an unethical and unsocial set-up. It is, thereby, thought to have not at all contributed to a sound healthy socio-individual relationship. The Cārvāka stand on morality has already been dealt with. It is indicated that the logical implication of the Cārvāka stand on morality is not transcendental but empirical. It is firmly rooted on socio-empiric foundation, being pragmatically designed and without groping for any fanciful and visionary idealism. There is no attempt to treat morality and spirituality on the same par, but to treat them as different from each other. In other words, there is no necessary relation between the two. In what follows an attempt shall be made to expose the logical significance of the Cārvāka stand on the socio-individual relationship, basing upon certain stray references that are available in different corners.

I. The Vedic *Yajña*

It is said that a sure and certain silver-coin is preferable to a dubious gold coin[1]. The contextual implication is, whatever is practically useful, efficacious and quite sound in retaining socio-individual transaction is desirable. There is no reasonable sense of pining for some trans-social, trans-empirical, spiritual state of perfection. Whatever moral sense is readily applicable and is conducive to socio-individual cohesion is preferred from the Cārvāka point of view. In this context, there is clear reference about productive manual work and also about intelligent step which are found to be necessary for smooth conduct of living both individually and collectively. All such moves are found to have been promoted and encouraged by that stand. Agriculture, trade and cattle-breeding are illustrative cases befitting to the then situation. Instead of craving for trans-empirical woolly sense of immortal soul, the concern for peaceful and just living within socio-human setting is emphasized. It strengthens socio-individual ties.

The Cārvāka stand is opposed to discrimination among individuals on the basis of caste, colour and race. It is clearly against caste/class discrimination of any sort. It is held that such biased and prejudiced distinctions among humans are based on dogmatic superstition and, as such, those are unproductive and upset socio-individual solidarity[2].

The Vedic protagonists, especially the Pūrva Mīmāṁsakas are emphatic on the performance of rites and rituals including sacrificial offering (*yajña*) of animals (and, in some cases, even humans). Those heinous acts are given religious sanction on the basis of delusion that the sacrificed animals would attain heaven (*svarga*) and the performer of the sacrifice (*kartā*) would attain the desired result. It

1. *Varaṁ ṣṁśayikānnickāt asāṁśayikaḥ kārṣāpaṇaḥ*" Bārhaspatya Sūtra (henceforth BS)-14.
2. *Naiva varṇāśramādināṁ kriyāśca phaladāyikāḥ*" BS -39.

is needless to repeat that such sacrificial act, in any form, is a gross act of violence (*hiṁsā*) sans moral justification. It is neither good for the individual nor is good for the society. The individual who is led to perform such atrocious act on the recommendation of the so-called sacred Vedic injunction (*vidhiḥ*) is rather deluded with a false sense of success (*siddhi*). Even the act of crime or violence is patched up with the assertion that the concerned animals are to attain heaven by being sacrificed. The Cārvāka's satirical remark, in this regard, is not pointless. Why not then, it is said, the sacrificer kills his own father (or any near and dear one) for the sake of his attaining heaven?[3]

The Cārvāka stand, in this context, is found to be reasonably critical against any tendency to escape the social sense of concrete actuality and to indulge in absurd self-centred solitude, neglecting the socio-empiric duties/obligations. An individual is born to a situation and subsequently has also some rights (whatever worth those are). He survives and grows in that set-up with his own ability and capability as well. He is not to shirk his responsibility and favour dejection. He is to face the situation and to improve, with his might, as far as possible. In that way he justifiably opts for this-worldliness and not other-worldliness. But, unwittingly perhaps, some Vedic as well as some Śramaṇic followers imbibe a negative attitude, avoiding rather neglecting family, friends and even well-wishers, for the sake of attaining self-purification and enlightenment which, as a matter of fact, turns out to be nothing but fanciful and esoteric. Such an attitude accelerates serious chasm between individual and social commitments.

II. *Yatidharma/Śramaṇavrata*

The advocacy for asceticism (*Yatidharma/Śramaṇavrata*) is a mark of negligence. Self-contentment is possible within socio-individual framework. As self-awareness is inextricably related with other-awareness, so also self-satisfaction and other-satisfaction are

3. *"Paśuscennihataḥ svarge jyoticmome gamiṣyati svapītā yajamānena tatra kasmānna hanyate"* BS -41.

compatible and are not opposed to each other. The sense of mutual bond between individual and society is deeply damaged by such ego-centric and pure individualistic temper. As already discussed, Cārvāka does not deny empirical self and his likes and dislikes. The ordinary person is normally self-conscious and validly understands a distinction between him and others. But that does not preclude him to have fellow-feeling and social rapport with others. There is no need to develop the sense of complete solitude in view of self-awareness, unless one suffers from some sort of morbid psychosis and is to pine for pure self-awareness bereft of everybody and all empirical accompaniments including his/her own body, mind and life. In this regard, the Cārvāka position quite consistently strikes a balance between individual and social self. In this context, the Brāhmiṇic prescription for relinquishing the family and the corresponding duties/obligations need serious reconsideration. So also Buddha's secretly departing the near and dear ones, by way of disregarding the social commitments, is notable in view of his wife, Yośodhāra's anguish. Some similar morally questionable instances can be cited from the traditional sources.

The Cārvāka position, in this context, can be logically explored, even if it is not overtly spelt out in the tradition. Such a position never promotes negativism. It is neither anti-individual nor anti-social. It rather strives for maintaining a meaningful harmony between individual and society. At least that is never unexpected from its philosophical view-point. It does not decry family life. It never directs someone to avoid social bond in order to make a dive into complete solitude. True, it gives importance to happiness; but never at the cost of others. The normal happiness that it opts for is not supreme happiness free from sorrows and sufferings in the absolute sense. It is a mixed one in which one's own happiness is primary not in the sense that it is callous to societal expectations. It is rightly held that Cārvāka is not a misanthrope but a philanthrope.[4] Its message is to

4. Prasad, S.N., *op.cit.*, p. 92.

keep one equitable balance between egoistic need and altruistic expectation. True, at times, it is difficult to concretize, but is not impossible.

This is very clear in view of its adopting a humanist (*Lokāyata*) perspective all through. As long as one lives, he is to remain happy as far as possible. This is meant not for one but for all. In this way, its stand can be rated as secularly humanistic. Tagore seems to appreciate this point in his view of life too.[5] So far as human affair or concern is taken into account, there need not be any unjust discrimination between dull and expert or child and old or rich and poor.[6]

III. The Decadence of Tantra

In certain quarters, an impression is made prominent that the Cārvāka stand is anti-social insofar as it puts stress on sexual pleasure (*kāma*). In this context, the message of *Kāmasūtra* by Vātsāyana has been referred to as parallel to that of Cārvāka. Some have read *kāma* to be the ultimate goal in the view of Cārvāka. Even some have found similarity between Cārvāka and Omar Khayyam in this regard. But, honestly speaking, such a move deserves a relook. For, there is no reference in the available source-materials that the Cārvāka view-point advocates for free or savage sex. Rather, on the contrary, there is clear indication that it concedes to normal and natural sex instinct within the civilized social set-up. Sex is a part of living (inclusive of human living) and there is no oddity in acknowledging that. To control it in the sense of full prohibition or full celibacy is something abnormal and it does adversely affect the human person both physically and mentally. Accordingly, to the Cārvāka stand, it seems, balanced and normal look at sex is not disparaged (of course taking due consideration of social norm). Normal sex is operative on mutual

---

5. cf. Tagore's saying that he does not want to die from this man's world *"morito chāina āmi mānaver bhuvane, mānaver mājhe āmi bechietei chāi"*.
6. *"Lokavyavahāraṁ prati sadṛśau bālapaṇḍitau"* BS -54.

consent and is thus different from rape or coercion. *Kāma* is never construed as ultimate goal but its due recognition as pointing to one natural aspect of living is not denied thereby.

But, all the same, there are attempts for some unwarranted extension of this point of view to excessive advocacy of sex, setting aside all sorts of civilized social norms. In some quarters, decontrolled sex activity is insisted upon by some later so-called followers who have introduced some paltry form of magical spell in some degenerate form (*dharmapatita tantra*). Well, decadence of noble view-points can be noticed in different socio-cultural traditions. Such unwelcome feature is usually introduced at a later period, adversely affecting the original noble setting which somehow becomes distorted and polluted on account of being taken up by miscreants who deliberately misuse the early preaching for their own vested interests. As a consequence, they infuse therein certain paltry tāntric formulas, combined with sexual activities. In Buddhism, there is the spread of Tantrayāna, culminating in *Sahajayāna* that abounds with unregulated sex, much away from the civilized social norm. This is obviously a fall from the original Buddhist noble message. So also the case goes with the *Vāmācārins* belonging to a limited portion of the Vedic fold, embracing the five left-hand tāntric rituals (*pañcikaraṇa* that includes *maithuna*, i.e. sexual intercourse) in order to attain the accomplished end (*siddhi*). This is, no doubt, a serious mark of fall from the commonly accepted social life-style, of course not in any constructive sense but rather in the pejorative sense of deconstruction. Such is also the case with the later degenerated form of *Vāmācārins*, called as Kāpālikas and some have mistaken them as the followers and advocates of the Cārvāka standpoint[7]. But the Cārvāka position, as revealed in different sources, never advocates any abuse or excessive use of sex. It is neither for sexual repression nor for sexual promiscuity. A Cārvāka, quite consistent to its original

7. Refer, in this connection, the remarks made by D. Sastri (A Short History of Indian Materialism, Hedonism and Sensationalism *op.cit.*) and D.P. Chattopadhyaya (Lokāyata, *op.cit.*).

tenet of positivist and empiricist stand, cannot also adopt any form of magical spell of attaining some mystical and ecstatic trance. Cārvāka is rather for balanced and composed expression, quite in tune with socio-individual needs and requirements without affecting the normal setting in any way.

IV. Female Discrimination

In the Vedic and purāṇic sources there are number of instances in which the position of women is drastically denigrated in contrast to men. Woman is belittled and humiliated only to be enjoyed (*bhogyā*). Nothing wrong is considered on the part of *devas* to indulge in sex-affair with any number of women (with or without consent). Woman is treated as a commodity that can be presented as a gift to the selected man at the time of marriage (*kanyā-sampradāna*). There are abundant references of sex discrimination which are still in vogue in one way or other in the Hindu social system. The woman as wife is glorified if she is chaste and loyal to husband alone (whether alive or dead); but a man as husband has the full freedom and license to marry or keep number of women as concubines or secondary wives. Husband is glorified as *devatā* and the sole role that is assigned to wife is to offer herself fully to him and even to treat him as God (*pati parameśvara*)[8]. Wife is required to observe fasting for the success and longevity of husband but not *vice versa*. There is no customary evidence where husband is to glorify the wife as *devī* par excellence and never similar honour is bestowed on wife by husband. Various types of unreasonable and immoral restriction are imposed on widow in matters of food, clothing and general living. Nothing of that sort is insisted upon widower. Is it not a glaring instance of unjust imbalance, causing radical mark of male chauvinism?

8. Śrīharṣa, Naiṣadhīyasarita *"īrṣyayā rakṣato nāriḥ dhik kulasthiti dāmbhikān smarāndhatvāviśeṣe'pi tathā naramarakṣtaḥ." -17.42* [Though both men and women are equal in respect of sexual desire, man (as husband) out of jealousy and vanity deprives woman (as wife) to go to other man; but he has the freedom to go to others (women) and this is sanctioned in the cultural tradition.]

In short, the Vedic, the Jaina and the Buddhist view of life at least in some of its dominant forms do not put woman at par with man. It is ridiculous that religious sanction is ordained for such sex discrimination. In Jainism woman is not fit to get liberation (*mukti*) and the dogma is insisted upon that she has to be reborn as man in the next life for attaining that. The Buddhist/Hindu/Jaina monks are required to perform strict celibacy and marriage, in any form, is denied to them in principle. But the principle quite often becomes inoperative, being practically unsound. It results, in some cases, illicit sex-relation between male and female, belonging to such religious institutional order. Of course, recently there are some effective changes in Buddhist religious practices and customs elsewhere (Japan) by allowing clerical marriage. Anyway, all such inhibitions and discriminate measures imposed on women are gross instances of unreasonable immorality. Those definitely have adverse effect on socio-individual relationship.

So far as the Cārvāka stand is taken into account, there is no reference for gender discrimination. No religio-theological restriction is put on woman as against man. A normal, smooth course of living, based on socially accepted equitable sense of justice without any discrimination between sex, class, caste etc. is indicated in the socio-empiric setting. The Cārvāka stand is an instance of secular humanism. It thus leaves aside any sacerdotal trans-empirical supervention. A reference states that the Cārvākas ridicule the hypocritical sages who enchant the Vedic hymns and move for performing such Vedic rites like *Agnihotra karma* to hide their own misdeeds like earning money in illegal manner, advancing for illicit sex-relation and taking recourse to wine.[9]

9. *Vide* Daksinaranjan Sastri's *Cārvāka Ṣaṣthi* in which there is the mention of Bārhaspatya Arthaśāstra (BAS) in which the following sūtras may be cited. *"Svadoṣaṁ guhituṁ kāmārto vedaṁ paṭhati"*; *"agnihotrādin karoti"*; *"surāpānārtha mahilāmehanārtha karoti"* BAS*:* 5-7.

It is, however, not well established through any documentary source whether such allegation advanced in the sources (and attributed to the Cārvākas) have some basis. But, one thing is to be conceded that such cases serve as allusion for regarding unfair earning of money, woman and wine as improper from socio-individual dimension. And, that is well acknowledged by a Cārvāka. He is also critical about pilgrimage[10]. That is based on some form of blind belief, fear-psychosis and religious fanaticism.

5. Gift and Begging

The Cārvākas are described as very much critical about sacrificial offering (*yajña*), gift (*dāna*), consecration (*dikṣā*), penance (*tapas*) and renunciation of the worldly attachment (*sannyāsa*). For those are, according to them, meant by the hypocritical priests to deceive people and get them motivated in order to give wealth to the priests in illicit manner[11]. Whatever may be the veracity of such expression as stated to have been told by the Cārvākas, one thing seems to be certain that the Cārvāka stand is quite critical about *dharma* being extended from socio-empiric human plane to transcendental supra-empirical plane of visionary state of being. Accordingly such rigid practices which are prescribed for the attainment of heaven/perfection are questioned. The Vedic sacrifices, as advanced by the Pūrva Mīmāṁsakas, are challenged not only by the Cārvākas but also by others including the Advaita Vedāntins (*jñānakāṇḍavādins*) too. In the socio-empiric frame of reference, any regard to discipline, honesty, transparency etc. is well acknowledged and there is no moral impropriety in abiding to all those in the normal human plane. The Cārvāka stand is not at all critical to such dharmic norms. But, in the name of acknowledging the importance of such dharmic prescriptions (which are socio-empirically relevant), if there is a surreptitious move to follow such

10. *"Na tīrthayātrā"* BAS -3.
11. Pathak, S., *op.cit.* (Referring to Rāmāyaṇa and Lokāyatavāda), pp. 156-157.

rigid practices to earn virtue in the transcendental realm, then obviously that does not stand to reason.

For instance, gift is normally expected for people, affected by natural calamities. It is a moral necessity to help the homeless, destitute ones, orphans, etc. But, when gift is demanded as a mode of earning livelihood or profession and such demand has an authoritative sanction from the scriptural and similar sources, then the objection against it is not baseless. Causing pain to oneself to attain some esoteric absolute happiness or quixotic state of perfection is definitely unacceptable from the point of moral reasoning. It hampers the social order (in which the individual has his being) to the extent that it becomes an indirect pressure-cum-persuasion on the public to follow such inhuman practices, having no plausible moral justification. All such moves are grounded on life-negating, other-worldly ill-founded empty aspirations. Clearly those are anti-social and those do not contribute to socio-individual harmony and integration.

Begging (*bhikṣā*) is glorified and is claimed to be an honourable practice/profession in case of mendicant/renouncer (*tyāgi*) on the supposed ground that those persons do not have any regular income (like that of being a tradesman or service-holder) but only those are to maintain their life in the modest, minimal sense and to serve the community by imparting to the people the message of spiritual wisdom. Such defensive mechanism for the continuance of begging is not logically convincing. By imparting so-called spiritual wisdom, the renouncer/hermit reveals their idiosyncratic preference which turns out to be visionary, containing least applicative importance in the concrete setting. They do not, in any way, contribute to socio-individual growth and development. Social welfare programme can be effectively worked out and implemented with tangible result otherwise. For that it is not necessary to accommodate the so-called spiritually accomplished beggars who are rather parasite on others for their sustenance. Yes, those who possess nothing eventually and have no one to support, need help and assistance for survival. This is human necessity and need not be evaded. On humanitarian ground, people from anywhere come forward to help such destitute ones, irrespective of caste, colour and race. But this need not be construed as a permanent source of help in form of regular income without any work in return. Once one is brought to normalcy, he is to stand on his own leg to earn for himself in the socially approved manner by utilizing his talent/merit (whatever worth it is). But the case of begging as a form of livelihood, earmarked for a specific group/class is never justifiable. It has no socio-moral foundation. The Cārvāka position, in this context, seems to be quite clear. That does not support begging in any form. It gives due emphasis on manual and other technical works which have pragmatic utility and are practically efficacious, without having any socio-moral lapse.

VI. The Concept of *Guru*

In the Vedic tradition, there is wide adoration of *guru.* He is supposed to be an expert in imparting knowledge, especially in religious and other fields. The *Skanda Purāṇa* (which is one of the major eighteen purāṇas) has a section called *'Guru Gītā'*, in which *guru* is given a special status and with that some authority (*adhikāra*) is bestowed on him, in contrast to the disciple (*śiśya*).The sense of adoration and devotion are showered upon him to the extent that there is one popular saying (particularly among the elites) which carries the sense among the mass to glorify *guru* in all superlative manner.[12] The saying suggests that *guru* is not only Brahmā/Viṣṇu/Maheśvara but is direct *Paraṁ Brahman* (the ultimate monotheistic Lord). Of course, such types of paying respect and adoration to the group of people who carry mentorship almost as a profession remain continued even today. One illustrious example is the celebration of the birthday of Dr. S. Radhakrishnan (Professor of Philosophy and one of the greatest exponents of Indian philosophy and religion in

12. *Gururbrahmā, gururviṣṇu, gururdeva maheśvara, guruḥ sākṣāt paraṁbrahma tasmai śrīgurave namaḥ.*

the last century, besides being the President of India) which is observed as *gurudivas* and students in schools and colleges adore their respective teachers. There is a general impression created in the public platform that teaching, in any form, is a noble profession and that is how *gurus* are mostly respected.

Such a form of paying respect to *guru* is quite innocuous. But, certain misleading impression is drawn from this in certain circle that *guru*, because of his unique status, deserves a sense of authority which should not be questioned and should be fervently accepted with a sense of reverence. Such an outcome is not reasonably sound. There are number of *gurus* who either do not deserve that sense of authority or they misuse that sense to such an extent that when exposed, they are ridiculed. Secondly, on account of conferring a sense of authority some sort of personality cult has been created around *guru*, suggesting thereby that his words are final, his views are unchallengeable. As such, he is as great as the ultimate Lord. Even, in some cases, without investigating on the words or views pronounced by *guru*, followers/fans and public in general are made to accept those with reverence as the mark of wisdom. The very expression '*Guru Bhakti*' does suggest that such type of unconditional acceptance of *guru* is most unconvincing. Particularly, in the religious circle, there is the rise of some expositors (*pravaktā*) who, by way of exposing their respective religious sayings and sermons, make use of their cleverly skill to influence the listeners to accept the sermons, etc. unquestionably without any doubt. Even any doubt or question is castigated as negative and most unreasonably is ignored as irrelevant.

In that way, personality cult of *guru* tradition has given rise to follow one blind tradition. The very simple word of caution and insight is to be noted that a *guru* is to be respected not because he is *guru* but he is reasonable. He, as *guru*, is identified as the person who has brought out that point/skill initially. In other words, it is the contents of *guru*'s saying or work that is important in this case, not his personality. If the valuable word/skill is imparted not from a professional teacher but from a novice or even a naive person, then also that can be attended to irrespective of his personal record or data. That means, it is not the person but concerned achievement that is, as a matter of fact, taken into account to come to a decision in the matter.

But, somehow or other, this important point has not been duly considered and uncalled for emphasis is laid upon person instead of his contribution (whether sound or unsound) and he is adored more on emotional than on rational front. This has led into blind and dogmatic acceptance of *guru* and elevating him to the status of divine Lord. Such an ill-founded tradition has been continuing in some religious circle to the extent that no question or point of clarification is ever entertained about the sayings of *guru*. Those are treated as gospel truth of wisdom. What a caricature or mockery of wisdom, it is!

But, despite the personality cult of *guru* being widely spread, one comes across number of instances, even within the tradition, where definitely conspicuous attention is drawn to the reasoned words/works of the concerned person, instead of blindly elevating him as Lord. There are references in the Buddhist sources which state that Buddha expressed that "Just as wise men test a claim to be gold by burning, cutting and rubbing on a touchstone, my statements, O monks, should be accepted after examination and not out of respect for me".[13] In *Bh. Gītā*, there is also a reference[14] about Kṛṣṇa's direction to Arjuna at last which has some affinity with the saying of Buddha. Kṛṣṇa tells to Arjuna to judge and decide, all by *himself*,

13. *"Tāpaccheda ca nikasāt suvarṇaṁ eva paṇḍitaiḥ, parīkṣa bhikṣavo grāhyaṁ madvaco, na tu gauravāt"*- Tattvasaṅgarha, 3588. For details see V. Bhattacharya, The Basic Conception of Buddhism, Calcutta: 1934, p. 11, fn.9 and K.N. Jayatilleke, Early Buddhist Theory of Knowledge, Delhi: MLBD, 1980, p. 91.
14. *"Iti te jñānaṁ ākhyātaṁ guhyāt guhyataraṁ mayā, vimṛśyai tad śeṣeṇa yathecchhasi tathā kuru"*. Bh. Gītā, 18.63.

the future course of action. This implies that Kṛṣṇa's advice/suggestion (stated by him before) is not to be construed as necessary binding on Arjuna. It is Arjuna who is solely responsible to have deliberation (*vimarśa*) of all the advices/suggestions and then he is to decide for further course of action, all by himself.

However, the cited affinity between Buddha's response and that of Kṛṣṇa is only apparent. For, in case of Buddha, it is expressed clearly in a non-theistic, non-spiritual/non-material background; rather it appeals for the application of rational scrutiny either for acceptance or for amendment/rejection of his saying. But, in case of Kṛṣṇa, the option given to Arjuna, i.e. to decide the issue by him, with deliberation (*vicāra*), is virtually advanced at the monotheistic spiritual background. To put differently, the advice/suggestion by Kṛṣṇa has prior binding on Arjuna which seems to override the point of rational discrimination on the open setting.

In this context, let the Cārvāka position be now taken up. It does not directly supply any clear-cut remark with regard to the personality cult of *guru*. However, whatever is more or less accepted as the key-points of the Cārvāka stand, there can be a sound analytical deduction of some response to the issue of *guru*. Though Bṛhaspati is acknowledged as the *guru* by Jayarāsi Bhaṭṭa (in his *Tattvapaplavasiṁha*), Jayarāsi himself has developed a distinct point of critically arguing against the validity of all valid modes of justification (*pramāṇas*) including sense perception (*pratyakṣa*) which is not found in the *sūtras* of Bṛhaspati. That means, Bṛhaspati is mentioned by Jayarāsi as *guru* only as the starter of a view-point which needs elucidation, elaboration and even some modification (if rationally warranted). So the mention of *guru* in Jayarāsi's presentation need not be construed as favouring personality cult of *guru*.

As a matter of fact, authority is not acceptable as something absolutely final and inviolable. True, in the normal transaction, if somebody is found proficient in certain matters and his contribution in the related field is recognized as new and insightful, then his subsequent view or remark is taken up with seriousness, presuming his remarks as pertinent. Nonetheless, this presumption actually depends upon the view/remark that he presents and not on his personality. So far as validation is concerned, it virtually depends upon the reasonability of the concerned view/remark and never on the specific individual features or personality of the person and his past records. So the authenticity of any significant utterance depends upon the objective situational factors and not on any subjective credibility of the person concerned.

To put differently, a Cārvāka has no difficulty in recognizing a person on any issue on open-textured objectivity not on his subjective or personal status. Even a *guru*'s view can be replaced by that of a student, if that is more prone to truth and objectivity. Here, one is reminded of the popular saying ascribed to Aristotle, "Plato is dear but knowledge is dearer still." Putting so much importance on *guru* as a unique person to whom special adoration, devotion and worship are insisted upon seems to have been demanded more on account of some sort of emotional spell instead of any rational conviction. The personality cult centring on the concept of *guru* has given rise to subject-worship leading to some form trans-empirical divine theistic Lord that the Cārvāka stand cannot accommodate. For, it lacks objective reason. Such type of undue prominence on personality cult never contributes anything significant to socio-human welfare. On the contrary, it becomes more confined to person-worship than on any course leading to socio-individual progress in the concrete actual front.

VII. The Vedic Violence

Cārvāka's critical reaction to the Vedic sacrificial violence (*hiṁsā*) has already been referred to. In no way, the Cārvāka stand makes any compromise with that. According to that standpoint, the sacrificial act is an act of cruelty, based on blind superstitious belief and also the vested interest and lustful desire of its advocates. A civilized human society cannot support any act of unnecessary violence on the ground of one's personal whim and also on the basis of dogmatic belief/faith. In this context, some defensive remark that the Vedic violence is no violence is not rationally convincing. Even now, where there is the overall acceptance of the Vedic ritualistic tradition in a dominant section of the Hindu fold, sacrifice in a modified form persists, i.e. sacrificing fruits (either cutting or breaking it) before the idol. That also is inadmissible from the Cārvāka point of view on account of the delusion that such sacrifice would bring better fortune to the sacrificer.

In Indian tradition, the Buddhists and the Jainas are against sacrificial violence. Particularly, the Jainas are found to be more radical on this issue. They mostly advocate for total and unconditional non-violence. Even, some of the radicalists amongst them close their nose with a piece of white cloth in order to avoid the killing of small insects being moved into the nostrils. Some puritanical Vedic followers are found to be strict vegetarians as there is the scriptural (śāstric) injunction against taking meat and fish as food. Some of the Indian Buddhists are also strict vegetarians more or less on the same ground. On health or other circumstantial factors one can surely move for vegetarian or non-vegetarian food. The Cārvāka stand does not oppose that. Only it seems to be critical about religio-theological compulsion.

So far as the Cārvāka stand is concerned, it can be noted that the Cārvākas are not for any such radical/puritanical measure with regard to non-vegetarian food on the ground of any religious/spiritual injunctions. If, in certain case, on account of climate/geographical condition and betterment of health, non-vegetarian food is necessary, then it should not be prohibited. But that does not suggest, from the Cārvāka point of view, slain of animals relentlessly/unreasonably out of sheer fun or blind dogmatic superstition. For the sake of general socio-human stability and welfare, there need not be any radical measure so far as violence / non-violence is concerned. There is no moral impropriety, if there is occasional and required deviation from the accepted standard. But such flexibility is considered as proper only if there is dire need or necessity for the sustenance of socio-individual order. Any ruthless and whimsical step, in any direction, needs check. And, the Cārvāka stand seems to be well in tune with such flexible attitude which is both practical and reasonably cogent. The stand appears to be nearer to the scientific finding that living in any form requires constant warfare of germs in which the polluted ones are overpowered by the unpolluted ones. In that way, the individual in society becomes meaningfully accommodative (of course, not in the pejorative sense).

Before the discussion ends, let there be a pause. It is true that the Cārvākas do not advocate any social theory concerning socio-individual relationship. Nonetheless, the stray remarks that one comes across from the various available sources about the Cārvākas, indicate an ordinarily acceptable position regarding the issue. Classically, in the field of social philosophy, two prominent theories are found. One is social contract and the other is organic. The former gives emphasis on agreement among citizens to behave in a way that benefits everybody and the latter takes society to be one organic whole in which members are all organically related in such a manner that a disturbance caused in one affects the other. The Cārvākas do not clearly opt for any of the aforesaid views. Their position does not, it seems, favour for any such contract or agreement among the individuals to live in a particular manner and that is final and unalterable. Nor even, the individual is conceived to be an organic member of the society so that the relationship is construed to be not artificial but organic.

One thing seems to be quite clear that the Cārvāka stand does not entertain any supra-empirical transcendental *a priori* presupposition to explain the relationship between individual members and society. It does not treat society in some non-natural fixed pattern and the individual remains as a puppet almost to behave only in such manner that society commands or dictates. Freedom of the individual is not curtailed. But, again, there is no passport for absolute freedom completely setting aside the individual's normal and proper needs and expectations. Individual, at the same time, cannot bypass and defy the social obligation by way of any abnormal/eccentric or whimsical temper. There is need for a proper balancing device by means of which socio-individual relationship is oriented and shaped. Individual is not given absolute prominence. Society too is not viewed as overlord to be just abided unconditionally and not to move for any change or reform. In other words, both individual and society must have to be viewed on a flexible and dynamic procedure. And, in that manner, change or reform is open for individual and society as well. It is to be pointed out that society is formed for the benefit and requirement of its members and not otherwise. So, if certain rules and regulations are framed long before, at a different situation which is now otiose both legally and morally, then those are to be modified. Of course, thereby the entire social order is not changed to something trans-social and mystical. All the issues, raised in this connection, are out of pragmatic necessity at the practical front and, as such, those are to be solved/resolved in the socio-human framework. It seems that the Cārvāka stand does not ignore the role of applied ethics in this regard.

The Cārvāka stand fits into this perspective, quite consistent with its general life-view that is empirical and not trans-empirical. Debt is accommodative only on certain specific occasion and never in a capricious and whimsical manner. Teacher is to teach and guide student. There is nothing abnormal in it. But, if from this, a general trend is grown and is given accent to the ill-founded suggestion that the teacher, by all means, is the supreme authority and he cannot be questioned, even if the fact is otherwise, then that is clearly inadmissible. This is what is rightly opposed from the standpoint of objective reason. It is that which has to be acknowledged as the parameter and not the person, however great he is otherwise. Nor even, anything raised from the sector of youth must be obeyed on the ground that young has the sense of energy and power which the old is deprived of. Such an attitude equally lacks moral reasoning and, as such, turns out to be vulnerable for retaining socio-individual bond. It is rather based on the ill-based factor 'might is right'. The Cārvāka stand seems to be against any of the radical extreme positions and prefers to adopt a practical procedure for taking up that step which does not jeopardize the socio-individual system as a whole (for radicalism, in any way, leads to anarchy and chaos) but only to introduce changes and reforms which are warranted from the angle of the socio-human general moral standard, being within the empirical dimension.

CONCLUSION

I. Background

In the previous chapters, there has been the discussion of the philosophy of Cārvāka on major issues like knowledge, self, God, morality and socio-individual relationships. A critical estimation of the Cārvāka account as materialistic has also been dealt with. Perennially the philosophical discourse is found to have inalienable link with some form of metaphysics. The discussion either turns out to be positive or negative. It is indicated before as to how depending upon the scanty source-materials that are available on the Cārvāka view-point, it is found to be rationally not clear, rather unconvincing to characterize the Cārvāka point of view as propounding the philosophy of materialism. In fact the Cārvāka stand, as is viewed before, cannot be considered as supporting any form of trans-empirical, transcendental metaphysical world-view. It does not subscribe to any view about ultimate reality. As a matter of fact it is not committed to have any notion of ultimate reality. It seems, the Cārvāka stand is rather mainly averse to metaphysical stand.

In the contemporary philosophical circle, there have been profuse deliberations on metaphysics, both for and against. In that context, there is also reference about ontology and it is held in certain quarters that some form of ontological commitment is inescapable in any form of enquiry, be it commonsensical or scientific or philosophical. Some are found to be very much critical rather radical about the prospect of metaphysics, while others are somewhat sober by way of advancing a classification of metaphysics either as descriptive or as revisionary and thereafter indicating their preference for former (cf. Strawson). Again, there are number of philosophers who continue to embrace metaphysics as vital for the purpose of philosophic pursuit. Of course, the term/concept: metaphysics has been found as being employed in varied senses, at times quite different/opposed to each other. All this reveals *prima facie* at least some sort of impreciseness about the use and application of metaphysics. A probe into that seems to be all the more important in the context of exposition as well as evaluation of the Cārvāka point of view.

II. Varied Meanings of Metaphysics

So far as lexical source is concerned, more or less there is unanimity that metaphysics is a branch of philosophy which deals with or investigates into the nature of first principles like being, existence, truth and knowledge.[1] But, it is noticed that despite the general agreement there are some change and alternate mode of emphasis which are introduced in the use and application of metaphysics. While metaphysics deals with ultimate being/existence, epistemology is concerned with the nature and scope of knowledge. The concepts like reality and truth are taken up for philosophical scrutiny from the angle of metaphysics and epistemology respectively. The philosophical enquiry is raised in certain quarters about 'knowledge' and 'truth' independent of any prior metaphysical speculation / commitment.

Both in common sense and science there is, of course, the approved use and application of such concepts like being and existence etc. But the metaphysical enquiry of such concepts is primarily to speculate about their abstractness without limiting to any particular or specific concrete use of those in the actual context. For instance, it is not so much concerned with specific being like

1. New Oxford Advanced Learner's Dictionary (2009), p. 963, The Pocket Oxford Dictionary (1955), p. 495 and Chambers Concise 20th Century Dictionary (1991), p. 605.

human being /natural being /supernatural being but with being as such. So also the case goes with existence. And, in this sense, metaphysical enquiry classically is treated as philosophical.

But it is notable that the metaphysicians themselves do not have unanimity with regard to the nature as well as number of such first principles so far as their enquiry is concerned. For instance, though metaphysics as a study of being is taken up generally, in some cases, being and existence are not distinguished or kept apart. Being, there in the pure /perfect sense, is treated same as existence. For Parmenides, being and existence are one and the same; whereas, for Heracleitus, becoming alone is real or nothing is permanent. While for some essence is the ultimate reality or existence as such, others like existentialists hold that existence is prior to essence. It (existence) is recognized as the first principle in philosophic enquiry.

Heidegger, a recognized prominent existentialist, presents a peculiar notion of metaphysics.[2] According to him, metaphysical enquiry is about being. But the concept of being (*Sein*) is, to him, indefinable; though it can be explicated. He distinguishes between the concept of being and the concept of existent (*Sciendes*). But, again, for his metaphysical purpose he specifies a peculiar type of existent as the basic (as it alone poses the question of its being) which he terms as Being-there (*Dasein*). To Heidegger metaphysics is the study that goes beyond being and so deals with nothing. He ends with the remark that why is there anything at all and not rather nothing.[3]

2. Despite attribution of existentialism to him, Heidegger held *"My philosophical tendencies cannot be classified as existentialist; the question which principally concerns me is not that of man's* Existenz *(existence); it is being in its totality and as such,"* Quoted by John Passmore: A Hundred Years of Philosophy (A Pelican Paperback), p. 483.
3: Heidegger *Was ist Metaphysik and Sein Und Zeit.* See also Ralph Mannheim: An Introduction to Metaphysics (Trans), New York, 1961.

III. Varied Meanings of Ontology

The term 'ontology' is similarly used both in lexical and philosophical circles not quite precisely. It is said to be a branch of philosophy that deals with the nature of existence.[4] In that sense, the concept 'ontology' and the concept 'metaphysics' are not kept apart. But, again, there is also the lexical reference that ontology is that part of metaphysics which deals with essence of thing or being.[5] It is obvious that in the former sense, ontology deals with existence and in the latter sense, it deals with essence (of thing or being). It is interesting to note here that, while for some philosophers, there is no distinction between existence and essence cf. Śaṅkara to whom existence (*sattā*) is essence (*sāra*)[6], the existentialists (as seen before) maintained that it is not essence but existence that is fundamental in their metaphysical position. But for Quine, for instance, essence is primary or prior to existence from an altogether different angle, i.e. of analyzing the conceptual framework without any metaphysical background. To him, it is the predicates/properties ascribed to a subject/thing (its defining characteristics) that become the crucial factor for the subject or thing in order to be existent.[7] To put differently, it is the defining properties or the essence that determine what sort of thing is to be accepted as existent. Strawson, who is well known in the analytical circle in formulating the distinction between descriptive and revisionary metaphysics[8], has used the term: metaphysics limiting it to the conceptual framework and not beyond that (i.e., for any speculative, transcendental reality of essential being or existence).

Logical positivists/empiricists like Carnap ("Elimination of Metaphysics through Logical Analysis of Language") and Ayer

4. New Oxford Advanced Learner's Dictionary, *op.cit.* p. 1061.
5. Chambers Concise 20th Century Dictionary, *op.cit.* p. 676.
6. *"Sattā eva bodha, bodha eva sattā".*
7. Vide his *"On what there is"* in From a Logical Point of View, Cambridge: Harvard University Press, 1953.
8. His Individuals, London: Methuen, 1962.

("Demonstration of Impossibility of Metaphysics") have, in their later writings, shown interest in accepting the legitimacy of ontology in contrast to metaphysics in the traditional sense.[9] Quine, who was originally associated with Vienna circle and later on has made a break-through in publishing "Two Dogmas of Empiricism" has also brought out a different account of ontology in response to Carnap.[10] According to him, issues concerning ontology depends upon the questions raised within the conceptual framework which he terms as either pertaining to 'category' or to 'sub-class' in contrast to Carnap's 'external' and 'internal' questions. Of course, he admits that distinction so construed is fairly arbitrary. In the ontological framework, there is the acceptance of all sorts of things like propositions, states, numbers, and physical as well as mental entities, even mythological entities. This is not something unusual. One may include therein both natural and supernatural thing/being for different purposes. But from this it is not necessary to suppose that such acceptance of entities in the linguistic framework is only a matter of preference (at the personal/group level). Rather one may, as Ayer thinks, find it convenient to include all sorts of entities within the ontological set up without any commitment to believe in their existence.[11] In other words, despite their differences on specific technical matters they seem to have a general sense of unanimity that ontological issues are not necessarily about metaphysical essence/existence of things or beings in any supra-normal /supernatural quixotic realm of transcendence. In any discourse (be it concerned with humanities/natural or social sciences), there is the

---

9. Carnap *"Empiricism, Semantics and Ontology"* in Revue International de Philosophie, 1950 and Ayer *"What There Must Be"* in his Metaphysics and Common Sense, London: Macmillan, 1973.
10. *Vide* his *"On Carnap's View on Ontology"* (1951) reprinted in his The Ways of Paradox.
11. Ayer, *op.cit.* p. 52. This clearly expresses Ayer's view as a departure from traditional version of metaphysics in terms of existence or reality as such.

necessity of admitting certain abstract concepts for a meaningful purpose of communication as well as their functional operation. There is, of course, the involvement of ontological entities, otherwise comprehension and communication would be paralyzed. But, all the same, the belief in their queer metaphysical existence in the sense of complete transcendence is never logically warranted.

IV. The Cārvāka Position

With this brief survey of the concepts of metaphysics and ontology in the philosophical tradition, let there be a probe into the logical implication of the Cārvāka stand on these issues. It goes without saying that there is absolutely no literal (or otherwise) references available from the Cārvāka (or the opponent) source which would either confirm or disconfirm metaphysics or ontology in the position held by the Cārvāka as a matter of fact. But this need not alarm the philosophical investigator in pursuing his endeavour to explore the possibility of constructing/reconstructing the stand of Cārvāka from philosophical angle that would at least be not unreasonable. This is not a matter of surprise. Even when one attempts to expose and evaluate Indian concepts and issues from philosophical perspective, it is obvious and reasonable to adopt certain standard and philosophically established terminologies/ expressions. It is also important to locate to which of them the corresponding Indian ideas/notions fit well. So, in this sense, there is nothing *ipso facto* improper to present, for instance, the Sāṅkhya view of metaphysics, the Advaita account of epistemology, the moral philosophical implication of *Bh. Gītā* and so on. All the same, it is also pertinent to mark that such coinage is not forced or arbitrary. Of course, only on the basis of such coinage being applied from extraneous source, it need not be outright rejected. For any meaningful exposition of any issue on any affair, it is reasonable and practically necessary to move for such adoption, be it for internal or external necessity. Only, it is to be carefully noted that such adoption does not altogether dismantle the original stand under reference.

Rather, on the contrary, the stand becomes philosophically (at least) more sound and effective in the general plane of reference.

It is already shown that the Cārvāka stand (as it is commonly presented both from its original source and the opponent version of exposition), is found to be, in general, emphasizing on empirical knowability and it does not admit on logical ground any conjecture/ *a priori* assumption/imaginary speculation for establishing any entity or entities (things/beings) as trans-empirically as well as supernaturally existent. Critical remark against existence of hell, heaven, disembodied soul/self, *īśvara/Parameśvara and deva/ iṣṭadeva* is not only on the ground that such entities/beings are not sensibly known but also those are not cognitively conceivable. The scientific conjecturally construed entities are thereby not, however, excluded from the Cārvāka angle on account of their effective applicability on the empirical knowledge. The Cārvāka stand does not necessarily oppose the personal sense of belief/faith which is held on emotional and sentimental ground without having any cognitive knowledge/claim regarding the contents of such belief etc. Only the religio-theological claim that such supra-empirical, supra-natural beings or entities do exist either as the only real ones, or as far superior to the empirically knowable things/beings which are nothing but far inferior ones gradationally is contested.

In the sense, as it is discussed before, the Cārvāka stand is not committed to adopt any metaphysical 'isms', be it materialism, spiritualism or anything whatsoever. To put simply, the Cārvāka stand is rooted in common sense and it does not have the justified need to accommodate the elitist model which completely debunks the common sense framework. There is no difficulty, however, in improving or recasting the set commonsensical attitudes and beliefs by any other intellectual findings which substitute such thinking for better consequences at the empirical sphere with required practical utility and also keeping the general sense of socio-human discipline and morality intact. But, on the other hand, if any sophisticated move is ultimately directed to fully belittle the ordinary common sense as well as all varieties of intellectually framed and practically oriented enterprises including the scientific findings as chiefly self-centred, prudential efforts and, in contrast, to boost up some trans-intellectual, trans-empirical, visionary, intuitive, mystical experience as pointing to reality as such, then such a move is definitely parted with according to the Cārvāka position. For, such a transcendental state pointing to absolute reality is virtually implausible. Such a claim concerning meta-conceptual object of experience cannot be reasonably upheld. However, on that basis the technical objects in the scientific framework which are admitted on the basis of their indirect form of confirmability (beyond the ordinary common sense range of perceptuality) are not opposed. The religio-theological claim is virtually aimed at establishing the enigmatic reality of such beings/ entities even if those are not conceivable by the canons of reason and sense in principle. In this context, neither denial nor affirmation concerning the existence of such entities is entertained from the Cārvāka standpoint on the logical ground of reason (*hetu*).

The modern sense of different meaning attributed to the concept; metaphysics in the light of pointing to the conceptual framework as a whole and not referring to any meta-conceptual, transcendental, existential being/entity, mostly advocated by the analytical philosophers in general, is not expected to be spelt out clearly by the Cārvākas belonging to the remote past. It is obviously too much to anticipate that. During 20th century, there has been the rise and growth of phenomenology (not phenomenalism) in continent whose principal figure is Edmund Husserl. His interest is on philosophy of psychology. According to him, the genuine philosophical enquiry (among several others) is confined to phenomenology which is treated by him as conceptual instead of being empirical. Phenomena, to him, are purely intentional and thus those are to be bracketed off from empiricality whatsoever. Being intentional, phenomenal acts of consciousness or such objects are reduced to what is termed by him as 'intuition of essences' - the central focus of phenomenology. The outcome of such a view held by Husserl leads to the point that each and every sort of entities is constituted by consciousness. Such a reductive conclusion is found to be far away from ordinary notion of consciousness and the object of consciousness. Husserl's point leads to a form of subjective idealism which is obviously not tenable from the Cārvāka angle. Though it is admissible that ordinary notion of knowledge cannot accommodate a pure object of sense having no involvement of thought-constructs, it does not follow from that the object of consciousness is only limited to intentional objects and there is no valid sense of demarcating between consciousness and the object of consciousness as distinguishable in a significant sense.

In this context, the Cārvāka view-point that consciousness is not totally a distinct/independent entity but it occurs out of peculiar concatenation of different basic physical elements may be referred to. The critics have viewed the Cārvāka view-point (*Dehātmavāda*) as an instance of invalid form of reductionism. There is a legitimate distinction between body and mind, subject as conscious being and object of consciousness. This is very much in use in common level and also is found to have been approved in the general scientific domain. From this, it appears that any attempt of reducing one to another (i.e., reducing mind to matter or matter to mind) is obviously uncommon and moves much beyond the ordinary use.

But, nevertheless, attempts are made in certain circle to emphasize one of those as either more fundamental than the other or one being fully reduced to the other. The classical theories of spiritualism and materialism as two diametrically opposed meta-physical stands are referred to in this context. In the Indian circle, one comes across of spiritualism (*Ātmavāda*) in the radical sense of advocating the reality of *ātman* alone and all else as unreal. There are other forms of it in which reality includes both spirit and matter; although treating the former as superior and the latter as inferior. The opponents ridicule Cārvākas for reducing mind to body.

Consciousness is reduced to body and does not have any distinctive status. The modern exponents of Cārvāka swallow this remark of opponents by treating Cārvāka as a stark materialist.

But it seems quite clear that the Cārvāka stand is not logically committed to any form of reductionism. It neither opts for the metaphysics of spiritualism nor for materialism. The saying that consciousness emerges out of peculiar concatenation of basic physical elements is not based on *a priori* presupposition but is on empirical ground. It does not assert thereby any meta-physical reality of the physical element in the sense of trans-empiric existence of absolute transcendence. It, however, does claim the existence of physical elements as basic. But, to be fair to the Cārvāka stand, it is perhaps legitimate to suppose that the meaning of existence in this regard is not for any speculatively constructed metaphysical real existence, but only for existence as ordinarily used on the basis of empirical knowledge of how objects of knowledge appear phenomenally. It always keeps the door open for addition and revision so far as the contents of knowledge are concerned; conceding thereby the strength of probability and never it has any expectation for absolute finality/certainty in the extra-ordinary transcendent metaphysical sense.

In this perspective, its view with regard to mind being originated from body may be considered. The ordinary distinction between body and mind et al is not opposed but is well accepted in the Cārvāka framework. But that does not suggest that it goes along with the Cartesian formulation that body and mind are absolutely independent substances/entities and the characters of each of those are fully different. In other words, the Cartesian account of the two concepts is purely a metaphysical presupposition on *a priori* deductive procedure, whereas the Cārvāka account is on ordinary common sense foundation having its link with empiricality. It does admit the ordinary distinction between body and mind of the individual person. Never does it imply thereby mind is to be reduced to body or *vice versa*. The distinction is acknowledged phenomenally and no transcendental independent, real existential status of such concepts is ever necessitated. At least, this does not follow from the logical foundation of the Cārvāka view-point. That mind originates from body does, in no way, entail the conclusion that mind is same as body or *vice versa* and the two are operative identically. It seems silly to infer that because the curd is produced out of milk; it is non-different from milk and whatever is applicable to milk is also applicable to curd. It is clear that the Cārvāka stand never opts for such identity between body and mind in the empirical domain.

If the sense of 'brute fact' or 'pure objectivity' is a myth, then equally perhaps the sense of 'intentional consciousness' bracketed off from empiricality as 'pure subjectivity' is enigmatically incomprehensible. A Cārvāka does not, it seems, commit to any of the aforesaid radical moves. It does neither subscribe to pure subjectivity nor to pure objectivity as metaphysically inescapable. It seems to be content with what appears or revealed to human knowledge. But never does it outstep for claiming that what appears/ revealed is ultimately real (existence/essence/being). However, from this it does not necessitate the conclusion that the Cārvāka stand sticks to the common sense/ordinary position as inviolable. It does have the scope for review and revision, if something different appears or occurs. In that sense, its approach is philosophically flexible, dynamic and progressive. Instead of pining for any mythical absolute certainty, it has the clear option for evidential probability (not in the naive pejorative sense). It seems, the Cārvāka stand goes along with what is elsewhere remarked that in philosophy, nothing should be absolutely sacrosanct: not even common sense.[12] In fact, any longing for absolute (in queer sense of metaphysical transcendence) in any enquiry is rather self-defeating.

12. Ayer, *op.cit.,* p. 81.

V. A Comparative Study

If all that is expressed here is found to be cogent, then one can note that despite its general empiric stand, it does not move to that Rylean conclusion of interpreting mind/consciousness in terms of some sort of linguistic behaviour by asserting mind 'as a ghost in the machine'. Rather, it seems plausible on the part of Cārvāka to admit the legitimate use of the concept 'mind' in the ordinary sense and acknowledging its empirical distinctiveness with all its privacy and individuality. In this way it, perhaps, moves along with Ayer's rejoinder 'An Honest ghost'.

It is already indicated before as to how Heidegger, despite of his being acknowledged as an existentialist, has himself disowned such characterization. This is very much evident from his own remark found in his well known pamphlet *What is Metaphysics* (*Was ist Metaphysik*) that the meaning of being is not the definition of it, but an insight into its essence. For him, it is clear that metaphysics is not so much for existence, as is usually comprehended, but for being as such which again is the very essence 'not in terms of what things there are but with what it is for anything to be'. Heidegger is for 'Being there' (*Dasein*). According to him 'metaphysics is that which lies beyond everything that exists'. Its task is to transcend everything that there is and its proper object is the exploration of nothing. Nothing to him is not negation; for nothing does not negate anything like negation. Its activity consists in being nothing.

Here, our purpose is not to go into Heidegger's contribution for detailed critical evaluation. Only for the sake of comparison and contrast with the Cārvāka stand this much would suffice to note that there is no scope for Cārvāka either to take metaphysics in terms of existence or in terms of being/essence. For, both the alternatives are based on some sort of transcendence from empirical concreteness and that is inadmissible from the Cārvāka view-point. Instead of explaining or supplying a seemingly plausible account of all that is there or all that being there, Cārvāka feels at home in sticking to what appears before him (in his sense-field) and applying empiric concepts thereupon he articulates/frames ordinary objects of knowledge (which is inbuilt with thought-constructs). Of course, this does not land the Cārvāka position either to be ego-centric or to be objecto-centric. It remains content with the common sense without tilting to any metaphysical side as already stated. So the dispute between 'essence' and 'existence' appears to be beside the point in Cārvāka's frame of reference.

In recent time there has been certain tendencies developed in some established philosophical circle regarding the indispensability of having certain presupposition in any field of enquiry (inclusive of philosophy) where some sort of conjectures/hypotheses are entertained for investigation in the respective fields.[13] Those are not sensibly derived or empirically tested/verified/falsified/confirmed (at least initially). If those are taken up without any serious obstacle, then why not accommodate metaphysical stipulations/speculations concerning the revision of existing set-up which, at the outset, appear to be quite awkward, improbable and valueless, but may turn out to be quite enlightening, innovative and valuable later.

As a matter of fact, as against the dominant trend of logico-linguistic analytical philosophy with general empiricist leaning, questions have been raised concerning the total value-free, pure objective enquiry advanced in the scientifically inclined philosophical pursuits. It is argued that the empiricists with analytical background have two basic assumptions, viz., for philosophical pursuit the issue concerning knowledge is more important than the issue concerning 'being' and, secondly, a clear demarcation is drawn between the

13. Collingwood, for instance, has maintained (*vide* his Metaphysics) that every statement that anybody ever makes is made in answer to a question. And, further, every question involves a presupposition. Referred to by Ayer, *Philosophy in the Twentieth Century*, London Counterprint, Unwin Paperbacks, 1984, p. 198.

object of experience and the value that is attached to it. With these two assumptions it is presumed that the logico-linguistic analytical empiricism is presented to be ontologically neutral and it is engaged in dispassionate objective value free enquiry. But, continental philosopher like Heidegger points out that such enterprise starts with the presumption that there are two classes of entities, i.e. subject and object. The subject is to perceive and the object is to be perceived. It is perception which is set to relate the two; but that is not just possible on the ground that one is a spiritual entity and the other is non-spiritual external entity.

In this argument, it is suggested that the problem concerning knowledge of the external world virtually starts with formulating demarcation between the knower-subject and the object to be known. Subsequently, a dispassionate value-neutral query is advanced about the object to be known. But that is just not possible to the opponents. It is not that the object of experience or knowledge is a brute, hard object in itself. It is already value-loaded. To Heidegger, knowing the world implies that one is already a 'being-in-the world'. In other words, the very sharp distinction between subject and object in the domain of any intellectual investigation is not problem-free. In view of this, there is recommendation to move beyond common sense and natural/social science. Here is the necessity to delve into metaphysics that goes deeper in order to search for one's own authentic being as against the usual common form of human existence, i.e. 'acting as they do' which is set to be nothing but 'inauthentic'.

In classical Indian philosophy, Śaṅkara Advaita initiates its stand (*Vide adhyāsa bhāṣya*) by indicating sharp distinction between subject (*viṣayī*) and object (*viṣaya*). To him, any coupling between the two though is practically necessary for any meaningful construction in communication, is virtually accomplished at the cost of comprehending the real essence, i.e. Advaita absolute (*Brahman*). That's why he recommends for transcending language and conceptualization. As Brahman is indescribable (*avarṇanīya*), attributeless (*nirguṇa*) and only transcendentally real (*paramārtha sat*), so also Heidegger's Being as such is trans-conceptualistic, i.e. beyond the subject-object dichotomy. Of course, for him, the Being as such is not construed in the usual substantive sense of pure existence of the monistic type. It is, on the contrary, held to be 'Being there' (*Dasein*) which has to consent to its finitude in 'being-in-the world' (ego) amidst the finite objects of experience and that is the state of inauthentic living. This sort of inauthentic state can be removed by the sense of freedom in man, through the feeling of anxiety (*angst*) of death and its capacity to live authentically. But agreeing to exist as finite, being-in-the world it succumbs to imperfect existence and that is inauthentic. The individual's relations with the world is the existent itself and apart from that - nothing. Thus metaphysics, according to him, is concerned with the study that transcends being and points to nothing. In that way, Heidegger's *Dasein* is neither identified with being nor with existence. It is evident that in Śaṅkara Advaita there is no scope for the admittance of nothing to be felt out of anxiety of death; since it is held that the individual self (*jīva*) is essentially Brahman itself and the realization of that is not on account of death but rather attaining eternal existence or immortality (*amṛtatva*).

VI. Observation

Since the Cārvāka stand is found as close to empiricism in general, it owes an explanation to counteract such opposing remarks. It is already hinted that any enquiry is rooted with some sort of initial presumption, which is not proved. But, nonetheless, the presumption is usually entertained with the supposition that it is true until it is proved or shown not to be true. But if the presumption is proved to be false, then it is withdrawn. Such type of supposition is quite common both in common sense and in scientific plane. Presupposition, though generally resembles presumption, is found to have its use at times strikingly on a different note. It occurs when one believes something to be true and uses it as the beginning of the argument even though it has not been proved. For instance, in the religio-theological circle, it is presupposed that the world is created and on the basis of that it is argued that there must be God as the creator of the world. The creationist does not wait for the presupposition to be disproved. Rather, it pre-assumes God as the creator on the basis of his prior belief, irrespective of the fact whether it is proved or disproved. In fact, for such a believer, the presupposition is self-proved and, as such, there is no occasion for its disproof.

A Cārvāka, being firmly based on reason, cannot obviously accept anything on the basis of mere belief unless and until it has some support from the core of induction and rational justification. The belief, however emotionally/sentimentally strong it is, cannot be justified as conveying something as true and imparting knowledge. Here, presupposition as supposition in the ordinary sense is not necessarily opposed. It is required at the initial stage to frame a position/view. But this by itself is not sufficient. It waits for further proof or confirmation from the relevant sources. The more it is corroborated by different evidential and justified ground it becomes strengthened and more probable. But, when the presupposition is just taken for granted as a matter of strong faith or belief without it being independently proved or confirmed, it cannot have claim for imparting knowledge. It only turns out to be dogmatic.

It is held that any theory or view-point starts with some presupposition. Exception is, however, noticed among philosophers like Husserl and Heidegger who, at one stage, have searched for a philosophy without presupposition. As indicated, the views held in common sense, natural and social sciences are also said to be not immune from presupposition. Any required assumption/conjecture is not, however, necessarily avoided by the Cārvāka stand. Only what it needs, at the cognitive field, is a point of justification/confirmation of such issues on the basis of reason and not dogma. It is true that there is no perceptual knowledge of brute fact or object. As hinted earlier, the object of knowledge is imbedded with thought-construct. But that does not imply necessarily that we are simply confined to the object as valued in this way or that way. There is a perfect sense of intelligibility in which one can reasonably distinguish between the content of perceptual knowledge of the object in itself and the value or importance that is attached to that. It is obvious that there is a logical distinction between 'X is a man' and 'X is a good man'. Though values are applied to the concrete cases of persons (their actions and decisions) and also to events and states-of-affair, the values are of different type due to the extraneous factors like belonging to either personal or intra-personal sources. It is, of course, the case that values are manifold. The moral value, for instance, is clearly different from commercial value of gain and profit. In any case, the attempt to entangle fact with value seems to be not logically indispensable.

Some feel that the empiricist is committed to a position that is ontologically free. It is not clear as to whom this attribution is pointed at. It seems to me that empiricism (either logical or psychological or anything else) is not necessarily obliged to have a stand that is free of ontology. On the contrary, some sort of initial presumption/ assumption is well admitted at the starting point in any philosophical pursuit. But that is never assumed to be inviolable in any *a priori* sense. The sense of openness and flexibility is very much there; only that can be advanced with sufficient reason and justification. The difficulty, however, starts only when one jumbles up wittingly or unwittingly metaphysics with ontology. Cārvāka, being empiricist, need not confuse between the two.

Ontological priorities are admitted without any metaphysical obligation or commitment. For instance, the common man's notion that the world consists of human beings, animals, creatures, insects, physical things and manifold natural events and occurrences etc. is not necessarily grounded on any prior ontological theorization. He accepts such objects/events/occurrences as phenomenally real without any ontological presupposition of their pure existence. The scientists start with some conjectures to carry out investigation in their respective fields not necessarily committing to some form of ontological existence. In philosophy too, when one switches over to place some concepts as basic and putting other concepts to periphery and accordingly tries to give an account of the whole conceptual framework, what he advocates, is not concerning existential ontology but about conceptual ontology. And, in this sense, his position even if is characterized as a form of revisionary metaphysics, needs to be clearly distinguished from the classical notion of metaphysics in terms of being/essence/existence. The assertion that the thing has to be described in some way before the question of its ontological status can be significantly raised is precisely a conceptual issue and not a metaphysical issue of pure existence in the ultimate sense. It seems, therefore, pertinent to note the distinction between different types of ontologies like existential, conceptual, linguistic and valuational. All those can be meaningfully employed to serve their respective modus operandi. There may be occasion for their limited confluence; but that does not invalidate their distinctiveness.

In the philosophical circle, however, the meaning of the term: metaphysics and ontology have never been uniform. Different philosophers in various ages have shown inclination for providing divergent meaning to these concepts to suit their respective purposes. The concept: ontology was not clearly brought out in the early philosophical writings. For instance, Aristotle calls metaphysics as 'First Principle'. Collingwood tries to bring from it two definitions of metaphysics, i.e. 'science of pure being' or 'science which deals with the presuppositions underlying ordinary science'.[14] There is conspicuous difference between Strawson's account of descriptive and revisionary metaphysics at one hand and Heidegger's account of metaphysics of *Dasein* at the other.

14. *Ibid.,* p. 197.

Amidst all these differences, to bring to focus and to pin point the Cārvāka stand on metaphysics and ontology seem to be not an easy task. As already discussed before, the Cārvākas are critical about metaphysics. But the question remains as to the sense in which metaphysics is not entertained in the Cārvāka framework. If metaphysics is only confined to assert the trans-empirical/transcendental pure being/essence/existence as ultimately real, then such assertive claim of metaphysics is never conceded. Any trans-empirical claim of existence is ruled out. Metaphysics, in this sense, is repudiated. But, if it is meant as referring to the conceptual frame of reference (in which language in any form is involved) without any visionary speculation about the existence of trans-empirical/trans-natural things and beings, then that is not rejected *ipso facto*. Of course, such views or reviews/constructing or reconstructing/grouping or regrouping of concepts can be entertained only insofar as those are reasonably necessary. In any case, such type of conceptual mapping or survey is never construed as fixed and final, but as flexible and is prone for relook and revision. Metaphysics in the sense of probing and exploring the conceptual framework is not avoided. But, one thing seems to be insisted from the Cārvāka stand, that such type of enquiry must have empirical footing. Even though, concepts are not sense-originated, those are meaningfully applied and operated in the background of empirical phenomena. In that way, the Cārvāka stand more or less seems to remain within the domain of metaphysics of logico-linguistic empiricism.

With regard to ontology, the Cārvāka position can also be viewed as not negative. It admits the four physical elements as basic. It holds that any novel, emergent thing or being that is made possible due to the combination of such elements (in different proportion) is not permanent in the ultimate sense and it is found as being reduced back to the basic elements. All such claims are based on an empirical view about the world and the life that is quite close to common ordinary sense, of course, not being recalcitrant to general sense of reason and logic. Though the Lokāyata's subsequent development (admitting inference (*anumāna*) may also include ether (*ākāśa*) in addition to the already accepted four basic physical elements as also accepted by other Thinkers. It is notable that the claim of such physical elements as basic does not point to any metaphysical theory of their existence but only that is how those appear in the field of empirical knowledge. The logical possibility of some change of those in qualitative as well as quantitative structure is never ruled out and is always kept open. In this way, the Cārvāka philosophical stand seems to move on along with such ontological foundation that is not far removed from common sense and is not opposed to science.

SELECT BIBLIOGRAPHY

Books

Aiyangar, K. V. R.: *Bṛhaspatismṛti*, Baroda: Oriental Institute, 1941.

Ayer, A.J. (ed): *Logical Positivism,* New York: The Free Press, 1959.

---------: *Metaphysics and Common Sense,* London: Macmillan, 1973.

---------: *Philosophy in the Twentieth Century*, London: Counterpart, 1982.

Barua, B.: *A History of Pre-Buddhistic Indian Philosophy*, Calcutta: 1921.

Basam, A.L.: *The Wonder that was India*, 3rd edn. London: Sidgwick & Jackson, 1979.

Belvalkar, S. K. & Ranade, R.D.: *History of Indian Philosophy*, Vol.II, Poona: 1927.

Bhaṭṭa, Jayarāsi: *Tattvopaplavasiṁha* (*ed.* Sukhlaji Sanghavi and Rasiklal Parikh), Baroda: Gaekward's Oriental Series, No. LXXXVII.

Buhler, G. (*trans*): The Laws of Manu, Sacred Books of the East XXV, Oxford: Clarendon Press, 1886.

Chattopadhyaya, Devi Prasad: *Lokāyata*, New Delhi: People's Publishing House, 1973.

Colebrooke, H.T.: *Miscellaneous Essays*, London: 1873.

Cowell, E.B. & Gough, A.E. (*trans.*): *Sarvadarśanasaṅgraha of Mādhavācārya*, London: Kegan Paul, Trench, Trubner & Co, Ltd., 1904.

Damle, P.R.: *Philosophical Essays*, Bombay: Asia Publishing House, 1954.

Dasgupta, S.N.: *A History of Indian Philosophy,* Vols.1-3, (Indian edn.), Delhi: MLBD, 1975.

Dawkins, Richard: *The God Delusion*, London: Black Swan, 2007.

Deussen, Paul.: *Philosophy of the Upaniṣads* (*trans.* A.S. Geden), Edinburgh: 1919.

Dutt, M.N. (*trans.*): *The Mahābhārata*, Calcutta: H.C. Dass, 1895-1905.

---------: *The Rāmāyaṇa*, Calcutta: Wealth of India, 1892-1894.

Farquhar, J.N.: *An Outline of the Religious Literature of India,* London: O.U.P., 1920, reprint, New Delhi: MLBD, 1967.

Franco, Eli.: *Perception, Knowledge and Disbelief: A Study of Jayarāsi's Scepticism*, Delhi: MLBD, 1994.

Garbe, Richard: *Philosophy of Ancient India,* 2nd edn., Chicago: 1899.

Gupta, Uma: *Materialism in the Vedas*, New Delhi: Classical Publishing Company, 1987.

Halbfass, Wilhelm: *Tradition and Reflection*, Delhi: Sri Satguru Publications, 1991-1992.

Haribhadra: *Saḍdarśanasamucaya* with Guṇaratna's *Tarka-rahaṣya-dīpikā* (ed. Luigi Suali), Calcutta: The Asiatic Society, 1905-1914.

Hastings, James (ed.): *Encyclopaedia of Ethics and Religion,* Vol.VIII, Edinburgh: T.T. Clark, 1915.

Hiriyanna, M.: *Indian Philosophical Studies,* Mysore: Kavyalaya Publishers, 1957.

Jha, G. (*trans.*): *Manusmṛti with* bhāṣya *of* Medhātithī, Vols. 1-5, Calcutta: 1920-1926.

Kar, Bijayananda: *Ethics and Morality in Indian Materialist Philosophy,* IIAS, Shimla, 2012.

Kar, Namita: *The Humanistic Trends in Some Principal Upaniṣads,* Delhi: Ajanta Books International, 1989.

Kauṭilya: *Arthaśāstra* (*trans.* R. Shama Sastry), Bangalore: 1915.

Keith, A.B.: *Religion and Philosophy of the Vedas and Upaniṣads,* Harvard Oriental Series, Vols.31-32, Cambridge (Mass), 1925.

Krishna, K.B.: *Studies in Hindu Materialism,* Guntur: Milinda Publications, 1994.

Law, B.C. (ed.): *Buddhistic Studies* (chapters on six heretical teachers), Calcutta: Simla Thaeker, Spink & Co. Ltd., 1931.

Lange, F.A.: *History of Materialism* (*trans.* E.C. Thomas), 3rd edn. New York: 1950.

Macdonell, A.A.: *India's Past,* Oxford: 1927, reprinted Delhi: MLBD, 1958.

Mahapatra, Shastri, Pt. Damodara: *Sarva Darśana Śiromaṇiḥ* 2nd edn., Bhubaneswar: Odisha Sahitya Academy, 1993.

Misra, Ganeswar: *Language, Reality and Analysis,* New York: E.J. Brill, 1990.

---------: *Analytical Studies in Indian Philosophical Problems,* Bhubaneswar: Utkal University, 1971.

Miśra Jagannātha (comp.) *Rasakalpadruma* (*ed.* Pt. Banambara Acarya Sharma), Bhubaneswar, Odisha Sahitya Academy, 1964.

Miśra, Kṛṣṇa: *Prabodha Candrodaya* (*trans.* J, Taylor), Bombay, 1886.

Mishra, Ramprasad: *Sahajayāna- A* study of Tāntric Buddhism, Calcutta: Punthi Pustak, 1991.

Mittal, K.K.: *Materialism in Indian Thought*, New Delhi: Munshiram Manoharlal, Pub., 1974.

Mohanty, J.N.: *Reason and Tradition in Indian Thought*, Oxford: Clarendon Press, 1992.

Müller, Max: *Six Systems of Indian Philosophy* (reprint), Calcutta: Sushil Gupta & Co., 1952.

Negi, Surendra Singh: *Bhāratīya Darśana* (ed. in Hindi), Ghaziavad: K.M. Pachauri Prakashan, 2001.

Pargiter, F.E.: *Ancient Indian Historical Tradition*, Delhi: MLBD, 1962.

Pathak, Sarvanand: Cārvāk *Darśankī Śāstrīya Samīikṣā* (in Hindi), Varanasi: Cowkhamba Vidya Bhawan, 1965.

Prasad, Rajendra: *Karma, Causation and Retributive Morality*, New Delhi: ICPR publication, 1989.

---------: *Varṇadharma, Niṣkāma Karma and Practical Morality*. New Delhi: D.K. Printworld (P) Ltd., 1999.

Pulligandla, R.: *Fundamentals of Indian Philosophy*, 2nd edn., New Delhi: D.K. Printworld (P) Ltd.,1997.

Radhakrishnan, S.: *Indian Philosophy*, Vols. 1-2, London: George Allen & Unwin Ltd., 1929-1931.

---------: *Eastern Religion and Western Thought*, 2nd edn., London: O.U.P., Humphrey Milford, 1940.

Radakrishnan, S. and Moore, Charles A.: *A Source* Book *in Indian Philosophy*, Princeton, New Jersey: Princeton University Press, 1957.

Ranade, R.D.: *A Constructive Survey of Upaniṣadic Philosophy*, Poona, 1926.

Renou, L.: *Vedic India*, Calcutta: Sushil Gupta Ltd., 1957.

Riepe, Dale: *The Naturalistic Tradition in Indian Thought*, Washington: University of Washington, 1961.

Sadānanda: *Vedāntasāra* (*trans.* G.A. Jacob), London: Trubner's Oriental Series, 1880.

Śaṅkara: Sarva Siddhāntasaṅgraha (*trans.* P.S. Bose),Calcutta, 1929.

Śāntarakṣita: *Tattvasaṅgraha* with Kamalaśīla's *Pañjikā* (*ed.* Dwarikadas Shastri), Varanasi: Buddha Bharati, 1981.

Sastri, D.: *A Short History of Indian Materialism, Hedonism and. Sensationalism*, Calcutta, 1957.

---------: *Cārvāka Śaṣṭi*, Calcutta: The Book Company, 1928.

Sastri, T. Gaṇapati (ed): *Sarvamatasaṅgraha*, Trivandrum, 1915.

Sen, Amartya: *The Argumentative Indian*, London: Penguin Books, 2006.

Shastri, H.P.: *Lokāyata*, Calcutta, 1925.

Sattanar: *Maṇimekhalāi* (in Tamil, *trans.* S.K. Aiyangar), Madras, n.d.

Śīlāṅka: Commentary on the *Sūtrakṛtāṅga* (*ed.* Suracandra), Bombay, 1917.

Sinha and Basu: *Women in Ancient India*, Delhi: Khama Publishers, 2002.

Thomas, F.W. (ed): *Bṛhaspati Sūtra*, Lahore: The Punjab Sanskrit Book Depot, 1921.

Vātsyāyana: *Kāmasūtra* (with *Jayamaṅgalā* commentary) Varanasi: Chowkhamba Sanskrit Series, n.d.

Warder, A.K.: *A Course in Indian Philosophy*, 2nd edn., Delhi: MLBD, 1998.

Papers/Articles/Essays

Bhattacharya, Rama Krishna: "Cārvāka Fragments: A New Collection" *Journal of Indian Philosophy*, Vol.30, No. 6, 2002-2003.

Chattopadhyaya, Debi Prasad: "Materialism in Indian Philosophy" in *Knowledge and Intervention*, Calcutta: Firma K.L. Mukhopadhya, 1985.

Cintamani, T.R.: "A Note on the Cārvāka System" *The Journal of Oriental Research*, Madras, 1927.

Cowell, E.B.: "The Cārvāka System of Philosophy" *Journal of Asiatic Society of Bengal*, XXXI, 1862.

Gokhale, P. Pradeep: " The Value Perspective/s of Cārvākas" *Indian Philosophical Quarterly*, Pune-7, 2002

Kar, Bijayananda: "*Śabda pramāṇa* from the Cārvāka point of view" in *Perspectives in Contemporary Philosophy* (ed. Dilip Chakrovarty), Delhi: Ajanta Books International, 1998.

---------: "Ethics in Classical Indian Materialistic Philosophy" in *A Historical-Developmental Study of Classical Indian Philosophy of Morals* (*ed.* Rajendra Prasad), New Delhi: PHISPC, Centre for Studies in Civilization, 2009.

Law, B.C.: "A Short Account of the Wandering Teachers" *Journal of the Asiatic Society of Bengal*, Vol. XIV, 1918.

Muir, J.: "Indian Materialist" *Journal of the Royal Asiatic Society*, New Series, 1862.

Namai, Mamoru: "A Survey of Barhaspatyā Philosophy" *Indological Studies*. No.2, Kyoto: 1976.

Shesh, Prakash: "It is the Religion of Reason", *Times of India*, (Bangalore ed.), 09-8-2009.

Stcherbatsky, Th.: "History of Materialism in India" *Soviet Indology Series*, No. 2 (*trans.* H.C. Gupta), *Indian Studies: Past and Present*, Calcutta: 1969.

Tucci, G.: "A Sketch of Indian Materialism" *Proceedings of First Indian Philosophical Congress*, 1925.

INDEX